DISCOVEI
THE YOUNG
CHURCH

Dedicated to
our four children
and their loved ones
in their work of helping others
discover the young church

DISCOVERING THE YOUNG CHURCH

Gordon Moyes

Photographs by
John Graham

AN ALBATROSS BOOK

© Gordon Moyes 1989

Published in Australia and New Zealand by
Albatross Books Pty Ltd
PO Box 320, Sutherland
NSW 2232, Australia
in the United States of America by
Albatross Books
PO Box 131, Claremont
CA 91711, USA
and in the United Kingdom by
Lion Publishing
Sandy Lane West, Littlemore
Oxford, England

First edition 1989

National Library of Australia
Cataloguing-in-Publication data

Moyes, Gordon, 1938-
Discovering the young church

ISBN 0 86760 007 1 (Albatross)
ISBN 0 7459 1296 6 (Lion)

1. Church history — Primitive and early
church, ca.30-600. I. Title.

270.1

Photos on pages 37, 63 and 93 by
Georg Lindstrom, copyright 1978
Typeset by Rochester Photosetting Service, Sydney
Produced by Mandarin Offset
Printed and bound in Hong Kong

Contents

Acknowledgements

I would like to express thanks to my secretary Jan Fishburn for working on the manuscript of this book with me, Ron Schepis R.N. and Pastor Dick Hayman who helped me with research, to my readings, to Ken Goodlet and John Waterhouse from Albatross whose two previous books in this series have both won national awards, to Martin Johnson and the crew of Wesley Film Productions whose excellent productions in the three film series have won an international award for excellence, Rev. John Graham whose photographs enhance this book, and as always to Beverley who has supported me from the very beginning in all of our undertakings and who has made this book possible.

1

Peter the Disciple

In our lifetime, we have learnt more about the home life and environment of the apostle Peter than we found out in the previous 1800 years. This is due mainly to the work of a German Franciscan order which, in 1894, purchased some synagogue ruins from their Bedouin owners. They believed that this could be on the site of the New Testament town of Capernaum.

In Jesus' day Capernaum was a fishing and farming community stretching for half a kilometre along the Sea of Galilee. As it was on the main road by the border, it also had a customs house which is where Matthew worked.[1]

Many events recorded in the New Testament took place at Capernaum. After Jesus left Nazareth, he went to live here and began preaching. At Capernaum Jesus called the fishermen to be disciples and near here he called Matthew to follow him. His mother Mary and his younger brothers came to Capernaum from Nazareth to take him back because they believed he was beside himself.[2]

Many miracles were performed here: Jesus told Peter to find a fish with a coin in its mouth to pay their taxes; and in the synagogue Jesus preached and healed a man with an unclean spirit. He healed the slave of a centurion, who helped build the synagogue in Capernaum; he healed the daughter of a ruler in the Capernaum synagogue; and he healed Peter's mother-in-law who was ill.[3]

It was in Capernaum that Jesus was teaching in a house so crowded with people that four men could not get their paralysed friend to Jesus, so they removed part of the roof of the house to let him down. The healing that followed spread the fame of Jesus widely in the area. Here, too, Jesus taught about the bread of life and interpreted the significance of his death.[4]

Capernaum

Peter was a native of nearby Bethsaida, but later he shifted to Capernaum with his wife and her mother.[5]

The pile of rubble that the Franciscans found was a graphic fulfilment of the fate that was prophesied would befall the towns that had witnessed the miracles of Jesus but did not believe in him.[6] As they began to excavate, they were particularly excited by the third to fourth century synagogue which they began to re-erect. The basilica measured seventeen by twenty-three metres and was three storeys high. Beside it was a courtyard.

The synagogue included about a dozen columns which have been re-erected, and in the mortar on which the stone pavement was laid was found some 2,920 early fourth century coins. In the courtyard more than 20,000 coins were discovered. Highly polished limestone blocks looking like marble and painted plaster decorated the walls. The door

Part of fourth century AD pillar, Synagogue at Capernaum.

lintels, friezes, cornices and pillar capitals are delicately carved with representations of the Ark of the Covenant, the stars of David and Solomon, various trees, a menorah and many animals.

But the greatest discoveries were to occur in twelve remarkable seasons of excavation (1968-1977) conducted by Fathers Virgilio Corbo and Stanislao Loffreda.

Beneath the synagogue lies the foundation stone of an earlier synagogue built from black basalt from the first century AD. As there was only one synagogue in Capernaum, and as Jesus did preach there, this was probably the synagogue in which Jesus himself preached.

Then a more exciting discovery occurred on which the archeologists have been working since 1968. Just outside the synagogue doors were the foundations of a most unusual

Foundations of octagonal church: built over house of Peter?

fifth century AD octagonal church, an eight-sided church built upon an earlier smaller house church, and beneath that a very ordinary fisherman's house.

The archeologists found that the earlier church was built around two octagons, the inner one enclosing the foundations and the walls of the earlier house. A baptistry was built into the east side and the floor covered with beautiful mosaics including, at the centre, a peacock, one of the early church's symbols of eternal life.

Archeologists once more very carefully removed the floor of the house of worship from the first century and they discovered the foundations of a fishing family's house. It had been enlarged and the interior walls filled with rubble for a new floor that was laid upon it.

Whose house was this that had been uncovered? In the early fifth century, a Spanish pilgrim from Eteria wrote in her diary: 'In Capernaum the house of the Prince of the Apostles [i.e. Peter] became a church. The walls, however, have remained unchanged to the present day.' An Italian pilgrim reported the following in about AD 570: 'We came to Capernaum in the house of St Peter which is now a basilica.' This small house which used to be a house church belonged to Peter.

When those archeologists lifted the floors very carefully in 1977, they found pieces of plaster that had been covered for the last eighteen hundred years! The plaster still had some of the writing which had been written on the walls. Over four centuries the walls had been plastered three times and each layer contains graffiti.

There are one hundred and thirty-one pieces of plaster graffiti written in four languages. Jesus' name appears several times. He is called Christ, Lord, the Most High, God. Peter is mentioned twice and his monogram is written in both Latin and Greek. In another inscription Peter is called the 'helper of Rome'. Some prayers are broken but still meaningful: 'O Lord Jesus Christ, help...', 'Christ have mercy...', and 'O Lord Christ...'.

There is an interesting inscription from 3 Baruch 4: 4-15: 'The Lord says: "Bitterness will be turned into sweetness, malediction will be changed into benediction, and the fruit of the vineyard will become the blood of God"', a reference to the Lord's Supper which was celebrated in this house of Peter. Apart from inscriptions, there are pictures of fishing boats, crosses and a chi rho.

Not only is this the house where Peter lived: it is a place where Jesus walked. Matthew tells us that 'Jesus went into Peter's home and there he saw Peter's mother-in-law sick in bed with a fever. Jesus touched her hand and the fever left her and she got up and began to wait upon him.'[7]

Mark's Gospel has the following clue to the location of the house which has been confirmed by the archeologists: 'Jesus and his disciples left the synagogue and went straight to the home of Peter.'[8] The very word he uses means the home was hard by or adjacent. I timed the distance from the synagogue to the house and it takes less than one minute to walk. They came down the steps of the synagogue, walked across the road and past two houses and straight into the house of Peter.

The big fisherman

What do we know about the big fisherman? Simon, as he was known, and his brother Andrew were sons of Jonah the fisherman. (Imagine being a fisherman with a name like Jonah!) The two Jonah brothers, and John and James, sons of Zebedee, worked together in deepwater boats.

The Sea of Galilee saw two kinds of fishing: one in the shallows where the fishermen threw out a net and scooped up all the little fish, and the other in the deep where, using a series of boats like trawlers, they let down the nets to bring in a haul of fish. The most common kind are small sardines that are caught near the shore. One other fish is called today St Peter fish, which has a big mouth, large enough to fit a coin into, which might remind you of a New Testament story.[9] I cooked one of those great-tasting fish at dawn on a fire by the side of the lake and thought of Jesus cooking breakfast and calling the disciples to come and eat with him.

The call to discipleship

One day the brothers went to hear John the Baptist preaching. Peter, Andrew, James and John walked down to the north rim of the Dead Sea. It is a barren, flat area. The Jordan River provides the only touch of green in an otherwise sandy and stony countryside. It was 51 degrees celsius on one day I remember. The water is extremely salty, almost oily to touch.

John the Baptist said, 'Turn away from your sins and be baptised and God will forgive your sins.'[10] He preached a gospel of repentance and baptised people in the river. The four fishermen were among the crowds of hundreds that were baptised. Jesus also came to John to be baptised. It is eighty miles on a map from Galilee, but it is closer to two hundred miles if you follow the river as it meanders along the bed of the Jordan valley. Jesus walked that distance in order to identify himself with mankind's search for cleansing and dedication to God.

The next day, Andrew and another disciple of John the Baptist's began following Jesus. After spending some hours with him, Andrew found his brother Simon and brought him to Jesus. John's Gospel says, 'Jesus looked at Peter and said, "Your name is Simon, but you will be called Cephas"'.[11] The name 'Cephas' or 'Peter' means 'rock'. Jesus gave him a new name and a new purpose. It was almost as if Jesus looked and saw Peter with two different eyes — Simon as he was now and Peter as one day he would be.

The Sea of Galilee

It is interesting the way that call came to Peter. The German philosopher Goethe once said, 'If we just accept people as they are we only make them worse. But if we treat people as they ought to be, we help them to become what they are capable of becoming.' When Jesus looks at us he does not see us in our sin, weakness and debilitation; he sees us as we may become. He saw Peter as a rock instead of sinking, seeping sands. For centuries to come what Peter said about Jesus was to be the basis upon which the church was going to be built.

There came a second time, however, when Jesus called Peter to follow him. A little while later, the men had gone back home to Galilee and were once more fishing. This time Jesus came walking along the shore of Galilee and, calling them to a deeper commitment, said: '"Come with me and I will teach you to catch men." At once they left their nets and went with him.'12

A short while later, Jesus was teaching along the lakeside when he noticed the brothers washing their nets. He spoke to the crowd from one of the moored boats and, after he had finished, discovered the brothers had been fishing all night and had caught nothing. Jesus suggested they push out into deeper water and let down their nets, to which Simon said, 'Master, we have worked hard all night long and caught nothing. But if you say so, I will let down the nets.' Can you imagine telling a professional fisherman how to fish, expecially if you were a carpenter? Can't you imagine the response! But

Peter let down his nets and they hauled their nets in containing a great shoal of fish. When he pulled the boat to the shore, Jesus said, 'Don't be afraid; from now on you will be catching men.'[13]

Peter suddenly has a call to a new discipleship and to a new job. No longer would he fish for fish, but he would fish for people for the kingdom of God. For the rest of his life that was to be his occupation. For Peter that was going to require from him the highest degree of commitment possible.

The highest commitment

That commitment was to come as Peter found out who Jesus was. Jesus took on his travels Peter and Andrew, James and John and, by now, a few other farmers, a tax collector from Capernaum called Matthew, Judas the only Judean in the band, and a very politically active young fellow called Simon.

Jesus took them to Caesarea Philippi, the northernmost boundary of Palestine, believed by the Greeks to be the birthplace of the god Pan who replaced Baal as a local god. It was also a centre of Roman power, with a magnificent temple to Caesar crowning the mount. Philip, son of Herod the Great, built his capital here and named it Caesarea Philippi in honour of the Emperor and himself.

There could not have been another place where so much political and religious diversity was so obvious. This was the place for the disciples to reflect on the person of Jesus. So we find Jesus saying to them,

'Who do people say the Son of Man is?'
'Some say John the Baptist and others say Elijah, while others say Jeremiah or some other prophet.'
'What about you? Who do you say I am?'
Simon Peter answered, 'You are the Messiah, the Son of the living God.'
Jesus responded: 'Good for you, Simon, son of Jonah,' answered Jesus. 'For this truth did not come to you from any human being, but it was given to you directly by my Father in heaven. And so I tell you, Peter: you are a rock, and on this rock foundation I will build my church, and not even death will be able to overcome it.'[14]

There may occasionally come a time in your life when another person who has strength and character confronts you and you feel his life and strength coming into you. That happened to Peter that day at Caesarea Philippi. From the moment he accepted Jesus Christ as Lord, everything became different and his whole life changed, giving him new purpose and direction. He was now to fish for people. The big fisherman was born.

The self-confident failure

There were some aspects of the life of Peter that still had to be worked through. He was very self-confident and courageous. Every fisherman on Galilee had to be courageous. I have seen the sign 'Beware of the westerly whips' which is there today as a warning to fishermen. The early church loved to tell the story of Peter attempting to walk on water full of his own confidence and sinking. They also told of how he drew his sword to defend Jesus from the Temple police. These are frequently painted on walls and tombs.

Why then did such a courageous man fail Christ? Jesus had predicted that his disciples would fail him. But Peter said, 'Although the rest may deny you, I will never deny you.' You can see his strength, his determination and self-confidence. 'Lord I am ready to go to prison with you and to die with you!'

'I tell you, Peter,' Jesus said, 'the cock will not crow tonight until you have said three times that you do not know me.'[15]

But why should he deny that he ever knew Christ? He was not under torture, or even threatened with death by soldiers. A young servant girl simply recognised him.

I think it was his bravery that led him to follow Jesus after that night in the Garden of Gethsemane when Jesus was captured and taken to the house of the High Priest Caiaphas about 1.5 kilometres away. In the house of Caiaphas Jesus was judged. Then he was taken to Pilate's hall and judged.

Peter followed at a distance.

What takes a man furtively through the dark night streets of ancient Jerusalem until he at last stands in the courtyard of the house of the High Priest? I think he was there listening. I think he was there trying to find out what would happen to Jesus. He was waiting for some word from a servant or from a soldier. And while he was standing there listening, waiting, thinking — perhaps if he could rescue Jesus? — he was recognised. Then Peter denied he even knew Jesus.

I do not see that denial as cowardice to save his own skin, but as an act of bravery in trying to remain under cover. But Peter was no 007! When a servant-girl said, 'He was with Jesus of Nazareth,' Peter replied, 'I swear that I don't know the man!' and when challenged again, he said, 'I swear that I am telling the truth! May God punish me if I am not! I do not know the man!' Just then a cock crowed and Peter remembered Jesus' words and wept bitterly.[16]

The courageous witness

The Saturday after the crucifixion, the disciples were in the upper room. The doors were locked out of fear of the Jews. The next morning when the sun rose, the Son rose. Mary at the tomb spoke to the risen Lord. An angel said, 'Go now and give this message to his disciples, including Peter: "He is going to Galilee ahead of you; there you will see him, just as he told you."'[17]

Jesus was saying to Peter, 'I understand'. Whenever Jesus reproved Peter, he always said 'Simon' as if he were associating his behaviour with his old name, his old character. Whenever Jesus praised him, he called him 'Peter'.

That day Jesus appeared to them in the Upper Room; then he appeared to two on the road to Emmaus; to ten of them in the upper room; to eleven when Thomas came back and joined them; and then to a crowd of five hundred people at the one time.

Before sunrise: Sea of Galilee

Paul makes an interesting comment: he reveals that the Lord appeared first to Peter and then the other apostles![18] How significant that would be.

The impact of the resurrection of Jesus needed to be put into a context they understood. Where better to think this through than at Capernaum where it had all begun and where they had been so close to Jesus?

So Peter said, 'I am going fishing.' They travelled to the north of the Sea of Galilee and rowed their boat out onto the lake. As the dawn came up the following Sunday morning, a figure in the dawn light called out to them in the same terms as they had heard three years before: 'Young men, haven't you caught anything? Throw your net out on the right side of the boat and you will catch some.'

As they struggled with a net now full of fish, John said, 'It is the Lord!' But Peter jumped into the water and waded ashore. There was a fire on the shore and fish on the coals and the man said, 'Lads, come and have some breakfast.'

After they had eaten, Jesus said to Simon Peter, 'Simon do you love me more than these others do?'

'Yes, Lord,' he answered, 'you know that I love you.'

Jesus said to him, 'Take care of my lambs.' A second time Jesus said to him, 'Simon, do you love me?'

'Yes, Lord,' he answered, 'you know that I love you.'

Jesus said to him, 'Take care of my sheep.' A third time Jesus said, 'Simon, do you love me?'

. . . He said to him, 'Lord, you know everything; you know that I love you.'

Jesus said to him, 'Take care of my sheep.'

With each fresh question, one of the denials was erased. Then Jesus spoke his last recorded words to Peter which were his very first recorded words on the same shore of Galilee, 'Follow me!'.[19]

For the next thirty years, Peter was to lead the most incredible life as he followed the way of Jesus and cared for the young church. His home in Capernaum became the centre for the Christian thrust throughout Galilee.

So effective was this witness round his home that when Jesus gave his last missionary command to the disciples on the day of the ascension, there was no need to include Galilee. He told them to witness to him 'in Jerusalem, and all Judea and Samaria and to the ends of the earth.'[20] From the house of Peter, the witness was being made to Galilee.

For the next four hundred years it was to be the centre of Christian witness and worship in that area, and from there Peter extended his ministry to Jerusalem, Samaria, the Mediterranean coast, to Asia Minor, Greece and, finally, Rome. The largest church in the world in Rome marks the end of his Christian ministry, but the house church in Capernaum marks its beginning.

For personal reading

Theme: The making of an apostle

MONDAY Peter's home
Matthew 8:5-17

TUESDAY Peter meets Jesus
John 1:35-42

WEDNESDAY Peter's call
Luke 5:1-11

THURSDAY Peter's confession
Matthew 16:13-28

FRIDAY Peter's promise
Luke 22:31-38

SATURDAY Peter's denial
Luke 22:54-71

SUNDAY Peter's commission
John 21:1-25

For group study

Topic: Tentative disciple

1 Simon the fisherman was chosen by Jesus to be
a disciple. What qualities do you think Jesus
saw in Peter that would have pleased him?

2 What do Peter's responses to Jesus in Luke
22:31-38 show about him? What danger is there
in these responses for us?

3 At Caesarea Philippi, Peter confessed that Jesus
was the Christ, the Son of the living God. What
changes do we see in Peter's life after this
confession?

4 What changes would you expect it to make in
your life if you believed that Jesus was the Son
of the living God, as Peter did?

5 Why did Jesus ask Peter three times, 'Peter, do
you love me'?

2

Peter the Witness

Jesus had appeared to the disciples after his resurrection a number of times and had expanded their horizons immeasurably. What they lacked was the power to achieve. Jesus told them to wait in Jerusalem and power would be given them. How that promise was to be fulfilled would amaze them all.

A number of groups of Jews believed in the future outpouring of the Holy Spirit. The community at Qumran believed they already had received the Spirit of God, and they were waiting for a fuller outpouring of the Holy Spirit as had been prophesied. This would then usher in the Messianic era.

At the ascension of Jesus, Jesus had told his followers that, until his promised return, they were to wait in Jerusalem until the outpouring of the Holy Spirit would come upon them. In obedience to this, the eleven disciples, a group of women including the mother of Jesus, his brothers, and a group of believers met with one accord in prayer and waiting in the same upper room where Jesus held the Last Supper.

His open proclamation

Peter was willing to witness to his faith in Jesus in obedience to the last words that Jesus spoke to him and the other disciples: 'Go, then, to all peoples everywhere and make them my disciples: baptise them in the name of the Father, the Son and the Holy Spirit, and teach them to obey everything I have commanded you. And I will be with you always, to the end of the age.'[1]

For the next ten days these words, and how they would be carried out, were uppermost in their discussions and prayers. We read that during this time they were of one mind and heart and purpose — what they lacked was the power to achieve. That was to be remedied in a remarkable way.

Ten days after the ascension, there occurred one of Israel's great festivals — the Feast of Weeks. This was so named because it was held on the day after seven weeks of seven days since the Passover festival. This fiftieth day celebration, expressed by the word *Pentecost*, was a joyful festival marking the end of the harvest. Everyone within twenty miles of the Temple was required by law to attend, and strangers from many other lands would come to join in the one-day celebration. A sin offering, a peace offering and two loaves of unleavened bread were offered by the people. During the celebration, the people were reminded that God had given them a covenant at Sinai and had promised to redeem them.

While this festival was being celebrated, the disciples went back and forth from the upper room into the nearby Temple court where huge crowds were gathered. On this Pentecost, the crowds heard the sound of a mighty, rushing wind. Moving towards the source, they were met by a group of men and women who came rushing down from a nearby house, talking excitedly with everyone in such a way that no matter which country they had come from, they could understand them.

Those believers in Jesus were repeating what God had done in them, and in Jesus Christ. They were proclaiming that Jesus was the great sin offering for the world, that he was their true peace offering, that his body was the bread given for the life of the world, and that the whole world of people was the true harvest for God. They claimed that the long-promised Spirit of God mentioned by prophets like Joel and even John the Baptist had now come upon them.

Their leader, Peter, began proclaiming in the plaza with great boldness. They recognised that he was only a fisherman, but his knowledge of the scriptures, of their fulfilment and of the significance of Jesus of Nazareth amazed everyone.

One thing was certain: whatever had happened in that upper room had completely transformed these formerly fearful followers of Jesus into enthusiastic preachers of a new Lord and of their Messiah. What had happened, in fact, was that a new body of people was born, a new nation came into being, and a new relationship between different peoples of the world was established. Pentecost was the birth of the church.

Three symbols were associated with that birth in the same way as the symbols of the star, the shepherds and wise men were associated with the birth of Jesus. These symbols were the sound of a mighty rushing wind, dancing tongues similar to fire, and the ability of the believers to speak foreign languages.

The mighty rushing wind that attracted the attention of the crowds was the symbol of invisible power. Jesus had told Nicodemus that the wind was the

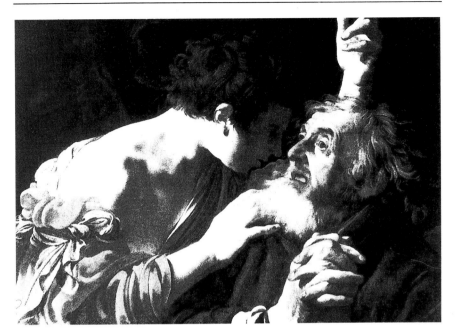

symbol of the coming of the Holy Spirit upon a person. It was invisible, irresistible, unpredictable, untraceable and powerful. The Holy Spirit comes upon believers as a source of God's inner power.

The dancing flames which appeared as tongues as of fire in the air above the heads of the early believers were a symbol of God's purification. Fire was used to purify, to remove dross, to cleanse a person from all that was unworthy. When God had spoken to Moses, his voice came from the flames of the burning bush. Now the flames would symbolise that God would speak through them with authority.

The speaking in other languages that the listeners could understand was not the phenomenon known later as 'speaking in tongues' — ecstatic utterances in unknown syllables — but the ability to communicate the essence of the gospel to people of other lands in a way that they understood from their own cultural context.

According to a rabbinic tradition, when the Law was given at Mt Sinai, the Ten Commandments were promulgated with a single sound, yet all the people heard 'a voice from the darkness'. They believed the voice went forth in seven voices which divided into seventy tongues, and all people heard the Law in their own language.[2]

Now, on the anniversary day of that lawgiving, 'each one of them heard the believers speaking in his own language.' They were amazed as they had come from round the Mediterranean, 'yet all of them heard them speaking in their own languages about the things that God had done! Amazed and confused, they kept asking each other "What does this mean?"'[3]

Hearing the message in their own language was the symbol of the future proclamation of the gospel among people of many lands. The Holy Spirit has been the source of the church's proclamation of the gospel.

Jesus had told them to disciple people from all nations and, on this day of Pentecost, he was giving them a head start by commencing the work on the one day when thousands of people from a score of nations would be present, and by enabling them all to hear the message in their own language.

Those first Christians now realised an important truth: God had equipped them to disciple the world. The two loaves of bread would represent the two communities of believers, Jews and Gentiles, who would now form a new body of believers, the new Israel, the church of Jesus Christ. A new kind of harvest began to be reaped that day, a harvest of believing people which has continued through the centuries until today.

From that day of Pentecost, the believers went out to turn the world upside down.

Peter repeated the facts about the death of Jesus and showed how it was the fulfilment of the scriptures. His death was well known to all and, difficult as it may be to accept, was necessary for the redemption of sin. God raised him from the dead and the disciples were witnesses of that fact. The Holy Spirit had been sent by the Son as he had promised. They were 'to know for sure that this Jesus, whom you crucified, is the one that God has made Lord and Messiah.'

The people reacted with despair and stricken conscience. But Peter told them good news: they could repent of their sin, be baptised as a sign of being incorporated into the new community, and they too would receive the gift of the Holy Spirit.[4]

Today, each Pentecost in Jerusalem, there is a marvellous scene at the western wall of the Temple. This is Israel's most sacred site. In a great area of open plaza at the Temple wall, preachers of the gospel of Jesus Christ from many lands proclaim the truth in many languages. They are hoping to see a repeat of that first Pentecost in the history of the church when Peter preached the gospel and thousands responded. On that day, of those that responded to Peter's preaching, 3,000 were baptised. With boldness he proclaimed that Jesus Christ was Lord. Peter became the first great preacher of the Christian church.

His healing ministry

In the last decade, a tremendous amount of archeological work has been done round the Temple mount in Jerusalem under the leadership of Meir Ben-Dov. This work has recorded that at the eastern side of the Temple mount was a triple gate which was the main entrance. This is the gate called in Acts 3:2 the 'Beautiful Gate'. Today, after centuries of being buried, we can see the magnificent wide steps made of dressed stone leading up to the gate, and still in place are the gatepost and threshold of what was the original gate. It consisted of three arches fifteen metres in width and height. Beautifully

carved stones from the gateposts have been found nearby. The doors were originally of bronze and famous for their workmanship.

As you stand by these arches, where the steps led up into the Temple, it is easy to imagine that day when Peter and John were going up into the Temple at 3.00 p.m. to worship when they were asked for money by a crippled beggar. Peter said, "'I have no money at all, but I give you what I have: in the name of Jesus Christ of Nazareth I order you to get up and walk!" Then he took him by his right hand and helped him up. At once the man's feet and ankles became strong; he jumped up, stood on his feet and started walking around.'5

He had been crippled for over forty years since birth, and was well-known in the community as he had a regular place at the Beautiful Gate. People were amazed and crowded round them all, and Peter immediately preached how the power of Jesus enabled the man to walk.

But the authorities who had crucified Jesus were alarmed that this man was publicly preaching about the crucified Jesus who had been raised from the dead by God's power. So they had Peter and John arrested and imprisoned for healing in the name of the Lord Jesus and for doing it on the Sabbath day.

The following day they were brought from their prison and brought before the Council of the Sanhedrin. They spoke boldly to the Council. There was little the Council could say, because the man who was healed was standing with Peter and John. They decided to instruct them not to speak in Jesus' name any more. Peter and John answered, 'You yourselves judge which is right in God's sight — to obey you or to obey God. For we cannot stop speaking of what we ourselves have seen and heard.' They could do little about this because the people supported them.6

They believed, they boldly witnessed to their faith and, as a consequence, a man was healed. Now Peter had a reputation for healing. The response to Peter was the same as to Jesus when people brought the sick, the possessed and paralysed for him to touch. They even sought to touch the hem of his garment. Peter was instrumental in healing Aeneas, a cripple who had been confined to bed for eight years. He achieved widespread fame when he raised Dorcas of Joppa, a woman of great faith and good deeds who had recently died.

He was to use his gift of healing rarely, but it was evidently a power given by God to help establish the young church.

His reluctant change

A radical wants to make things change and Peter certainly made things change, but he did it reluctantly. Peter was naturally conservative. Most fishermen, farmers and people who live close to nature are conservative by nature. But he became a radical, a reluctant radical.

The apostles in Jerusalem heard that the people in Samaria had received the word of God so they sent Peter to them. I am quite sure Peter did not go willingly. Why should he go and talk to the despised Samaritans? He was a Jew, one of the exclusive people of God. But his Master had told them to make disciples in Samaria.

So Peter travelled to Samaria. To go among the Samaritans and go among people who were not Jews was not easy for Peter, but what he did not realise was that once he started to mix with people of other races, and started to eat with them and have fellowship with them, God was going to do a wonderful thing in their hearts.

Peter went to visit a Christian in Joppa, the modern Jaffa. He was known as Simon the Tanner. A tanner worked with leather and handled dead bodies. In the Jewish law no Jew of faith who handled dead bodies could go to a synagogue or pray at the Temple. So Simon was an outcast. He lived by the seaside, as salt water was good for tanning skins, and because his business smelt so much it was not wanted in town. At noon, Peter climbed the stairs outside Simon's house onto the flat roof to pray. He became hungry and, in a vision, he saw a canvas being let down and in it he discovered all sorts of animals and beasts recorded in the book of Leviticus as unclean animals — toads and snails and rats and cloven-footed beasts and pigs. And a voice said to him: 'Get up Peter; kill and eat!'

Peter replied, 'Certainly not Lord! I have never eaten anything ritually unclean or defiled.' Imagine speaking back at God like that! But Peter was a conservative and careful Jew. Then the voice said again to him, 'Do not consider anything unclean that God has declared clean.'[7] How we need to remember those words when we meet people of other races, traditions and backgrounds. Three times that dream occurred.

Peter was disturbed by the noise of someone knocking downstairs. A Roman soldier and two servants from nearby Caesarea were asking for Peter. Caesarea was just down the coast. It was a beautiful Roman resort with a magnificent theatre, great public buildings, a hippodrome

race track, lavishly adorned temples and everything needful for Roman R & R — military rest and recreation.

Peter went downstairs and, when he asked them why they had come, they replied, 'Captain Cornelius sent us... He is a good man who worships God and is highly respected by all the Jewish people. An angel of God told him to invite you to his house, so that he could hear what you have to say.'[8]

First Samaritans, then a leather worker, then eating unclean animals, and now a Roman in Caesarea! But God was opening up Peter's life. He was learning to witness multiculturally.

So Peter went to Caesarea and found the centurion who was in charge of the Second Italian Cohort of Roman citizens. He believed in God. Peter shared the gospel with him, baptised him and many other people, and the Spirit of God came upon them all.

The six Jewish believers accompanying Peter were amazed at what God had done. This was a Gentile Pentecost following the preaching of the same message as Peter had preached to the Jews in Jerusalem. Peter had suddenly taken the church out of the confines of Judaism from being a sect of the Jewish faith and taken it to the Samaritans, to the leather workers and now to the Roman soldiers in Caesarea. Peter reluctantly had become a radical!

The news travelled fast to Jerusalem. The other leaders of the church were astounded. James was taking over as the leader of the apostles, for Jesus had also appeared to him, and his training

as a priest as well as his standing as a younger brother of Jesus gave him pre-eminence. James was a conservative and strict Jew and, when he heard that Peter was eating with a leather worker and then staying with a Roman soldier, he became upset as did the others.

To them Peter was breaking the Jewish law by going to these people. This problem of uncircumcised believers was to be the first big problem the young church had to face. Peter brought six witnesses with him, recounted all the events and compared the coming of the Holy Spirit upon the Gentiles to that upon the Jews. Peter's words caused them to stop their criticism and praise God for giving the non-Jews this opportunity to come to him.[9]

Yet that problem would grow in significance as God brought more and more people to the faith outside of Judaism. Nearly twenty years later a council was called in Jerusalem to decide once and for all what should happen between the Christian Jews and the Christians who were not Jews. At that time it was to take the wisdom of Barnabas, the logic of a Pharisee not yet converted named Saul of Tarsus, and the personal stature of Peter to win the day. It took nearly twenty years, but Peter changed the course of the Christian church.

Peter was the primary witness to the Jews on the days of Pentecost, and to the Gentiles at Joppa and Caesarea. It was Peter who was instrumental in seeing the faith break out of the Jewish womb which had given the church its birth.

For personal reading

Theme: The Spirit of power

MONDAY	The promise of power *Luke 24:44-53*
TUESDAY	The coming of power *Acts 2:1-41*
WEDNESDAY	The healing power *Acts 3:1-26*
THURSDAY	Power to all *Acts 9:36 — 10:16*
FRIDAY	The changing power *Acts 10:23b-48*
SATURDAY	One in the power *Galatians 3:27-28*
SUNDAY	A powerful life *1 Peter 1:13-21*

For group study

Topic: Bold witness

1 What brought about the change in the boldness of the disciples at Pentecost?

2 What was the reaction of the Pharisees to the healing of the lame man by Peter and John? Why?

3 Peter visited Simon the tanner in Joppa. What does Peter's willingness to stay with Simon, an outcast, say to you?

4 Peter discovered that the good news was for everyone. What implications does that have for the Christian life?

5 What does 1 Peter 1:13-15 suggest should be the attitude of the Christian to life? Discuss some examples of this from your own experience.

3

Peter the Missionary

The apostle Peter decided to live dangerously. He could have had a safe, secure and comfortable existence on the gentle shores of the Sea of Galilee. There was plenty of fishing for him there and opportunity for him to minister to needy people in Galilee where Jesus had been so popular and where they had wanted to make him their king.

But Jesus had called him to do more than just live comfortably. 'Come, follow me,' Jesus had said. Peter had followed as a disciple for three years. At the end of that time Jesus came back with a new challenge. 'Feed my sheep,' he said. 'Do you love me? Well feed my lambs.'[1] The acceptance of this challenge meant a tremendous turnaround in his life.

His first visit to Antioch

Peter visited Antioch, where the early believers and followers of 'the Way' were first called 'Christians'. It was probably earlier than the famous Council of Jerusalem because, while Peter was at Antioch, he needed to argue over the very issues that had already been decided at the Council.[2]

Peter had met with Paul when Paul had visited him for a two-week stay, three years after Paul's conversion.[3] Some fourteen years later, Paul again visited Jerusalem, meeting with Peter and the other leaders of the church.[4]

At this time Paul's particular mission was recognised as being to the Gentiles, and Peter's as being to the Jews scattered across the Mediterranean world. As Paul commented: 'They saw that God had given me the task of preaching the gospel to the Gentiles, just as he had given Peter the task of preaching the gospel to the Jews. For by God's grace I was made an apostle to the Gentiles, just as Peter was made an apostle to the Jews.'[5]

Paul returned to Antioch after his first missionary journey. He had been greatly troubled by the Judaisers in Galatia who insisted on believers observing Jewish customs before they could be accepted as Christians. Paul argued that faith in Christ was enough. Back at Antioch, Peter had learnt from his experiences at the homes of Simon the tanner at Joppa and Cornelius the centurion at Caesarea of how the Holy Spirit could dwell in Gentiles as well as Jews. He was now quite willing to eat with Gentiles despite all his traditional upbringing.

The old city of Joppa as it is today: a shadow of its former self

But while they both were in Antioch, a message came from James and other leaders in Jerusalem that they should withdraw from table fellowship with the Gentiles. The Jewish Christians in Jerusalem found such new practices hard to understand and a threat to their task of evangelising the Jews who might listen to a message about a Messiah fulfilling the Law, but who certainly would not listen to talk of people breaking down the old traditions and customs that had made them a unique people.

Paul attacked this attitude. He believed Jewish cultural practices were not necessary for salvation. But the Jewish leaders believed that while this was true, the practices were necessary for Christians to have a good standing among the Jewish community and be able to evangelise them.

Peter was torn between his new-found freedom of mixing with the Gentiles and the force of the argument from the leaders in Jerusalem. Peter was bluntly told to break table fellowship with the Gentiles and his old prejudices certainly found this more comfortable. He had an education that fitted a fisherman working on Galilee. We cannot blame him for not using his intellectual capacity to argue through the issues like Paul who had the advantages of extensive graduate training.

It was after this clash with the edict from Jerusalem that Paul wrote his strong letter to the Galatians over the same issue. But the growing controversy had to be ended by confronting its proponents in Jerusalem.

The archeologist G.A. Eisen discovered in 1916 an important link with the early church. While excavating a sixth century church he came upon the ruins of an earlier church and, within it, a chalice. It is a plain silver cup surrounded by an outer silver shell beautifully decorated with vines and featuring the figure of Christ with the apostles, including Peter.

The Chalice of Antioch

This was claimed to be the Holy Grail, the actual cup used by Jesus at the Last Supper. The book and film *The Silver Chalice* was based on this legend. More recent research resulted in the silver cup being dated from the fourth century. The nineteen centimetre high silver cup is obviously an outer holder to surround an important inner cup which may have been the original. But this cannot be proved.

The Council of Jerusalem

Although the chapter on James will discuss this first great meeting of the leaders of the first century church in more detail, it is important to note here Peter's part.

He was central to the whole debate on the relationship of the Gentiles to the Jews in the church, which argument came to be focused in the debate on the teaching: 'You cannot be saved unless you are circumcised as the Law of Moses required.'[6] Peter spoke first when the time came to resolve the dispute as was fitting for the one acknowledged as the leading apostle. He said:

My brothers, you know that a long time ago God chose me from among you to preach the good news to the Gentiles, so that they could hear and believe. And God, who knows the thoughts of everyone, showed his approval of the Gentiles by giving the Holy Spirit to them, just as he had to us. He made no difference between us and them; he forgave their sins because they believed. So then, why do you now want to put God to the test by laying a load on the backs of the believers which neither our ancestors nor we ourselves were able to carry? No! We believe and are saved by the grace of the Lord Jesus, just as they are.[7]

Then Paul and Barnabas reported all the miracles and wonders that God had performed through them among the Gentiles. The effect was powerful. James could see the force of Peter's argument, for every meticulous Jew, like Paul and himself who had tried to fulfil all the requirements of the written and oral Law, had groaned under the yoke. But added to the argument was the testimony of these three great men of God who had been blessed in their witness in the areas beyond Jerusalem.

So James summed up the decision: salvation was equal for all, fellowship between Jews and Gentiles was to continue and, provided there was no excessive disregard for moral laws, then

they were welcomed into the Christian fellowship on the basis of their faith in Jesus.[8]

Peter's strong argument and personal testimony was instrumental in turning the direction of the early church away from being a mere sect of Judaism and thrusting it into the mainstream of the Western world. Peter now disappears from view in *The Acts of the Apostles*. But that does not mean he was not involved in widespread missionary service.

Missionary journeys

Jesus had commissioned the disciples to take the gospel into all the world. *The Acts of the Apostles* outlines the spread of the faith along the lines of the regions mentioned by Jesus. He had told them to begin in Jerusalem, then to Judea, Samaria and the uttermost parts of the world.

Peter was to follow this outline of ministry faithfully. *The Acts of the Apostles* outlines the stages of the early church's growth: in Jerusalem, throughout Judea and Samaria, to Antioch, to Turkey, to Europe, and to Rome.[9] Peter's ministry, though not fully recorded, ventured into every one of these centres. The first twelve chapters of Acts concentrates on Peter, the rest on Paul.

The missionary journeys of Peter can only be surmised from conjecture, minor references in other passages, from his epistles and Mark's Gospel, and from tradition.

We should first briefly recap Peter's missionary journeys. He visited Jewish communities in all the areas where the young church developed with the exception of Egypt and North Africa. Judea witnessed the bold proclamation of Peter and John, and of Peter's journeys among groups of believers. Samaritan believers during a time of peace from persecution were strengthened by Peter. Joppa, the home of Simon the Tanner, was visited by Peter during a time when Peter travelled everywhere... Lydda... Joppa... Caesarea.[10] Antioch had been the coastal centre where the issue of Jews and Gentiles eating together had arisen. From there Peter returned to Jerusalem.

Asia Minor was to be the scene of Peter's next missionary journey, and he visited the centres of Pontus, Galatia, Cappadocia, Asia and Bithynia. These were all provinces in modern Turkey. This was to limit Paul's visits in the same area, because Paul had made a commitment not to work over the same area another had visited.[11] This was possibly in AD 51.

Corinth was another centre of Peter's ministry and a 'Peter Party' had grown up in this city following a visit by Peter after the church had been founded by Paul and before Paul wrote his first letter to them. This would have been some time after the expulsion of Jews from Rome by Claudius in AD 49, but before Paul's first letter in about AD 54.[12]

Rome had Jewish Christians in her midst from the time some returned from a visit to Jerusalem at the time of the first Christian Pentecost. Paul's letter indicates a large cosmopolitan community with names that indicate Roman, Greek and Hellenic-Jewish background.[13] After the death of Claudius, his expulsion order lapsed and the new Emperor Nero showed much promise. Peter visited the Jews in Rome in fulfilling his role as apostle to the Jews.

While Peter undoubtedly preached to Gentiles as well as Jews on these journeys, the Jews in Palestine and beyond were his main interest. Most of the early converts were Jews and this undoubtedly is due in part to the ministry of Peter.

Corinth with Acro-Corinth in the background

The writings of Peter

Unlike Paul, Peter was not an educated man. Yet what he said, when written, had a powerful effect upon the history of the church.

(a) The Gospel of Mark

It has been the unanimous opinion of the church over the ages that Peter told everything that he could remember about the life and teachings of Jesus to a young man, John Mark. His names were both Hebrew and Greek, so it is possible he was educated and bilingual.

One of the early church fathers, Papias, who was a disciple of John, wrote from Hierapolis in Asia Minor in AD 130: 'Mark, having been the interpreter of Peter, wrote all that he recalled of what was either said or done by the Lord. For he neither heard the Lord nor was he a follower of his, but at a later date of Peter.' Twenty years later, Justin, writing from Rome, also made the same point, as did Irenaeus writing from Gaul in AD 170, and Clement from North Africa in AD 180. To their knowledge, 'Mark handed down to us in writing what had been preached by Peter.'

John Mark was a cousin of Barnabas and with Barnabas and Paul went on a missionary journey through Cyprus and southern Asia Minor. Later with his cousin he went on another missionary journey to Cyprus. Paul had not wanted Mark to travel with him again, but later we read that Mark was a 'fellow-worker' with Paul.[14]

It was in young Mark's mother's house that Jesus broke bread during his last meal. Her name was Mary and, as a husband is never mentioned, it can be assumed that she was a widow. As she owned the house, kept a maid and it had an outer gate and a large upper room, it was obviously a house of some size and worth. It became the meeting place for the young church. Mark was probably the young man who followed Jesus into the Garden of Gethsemane, witnessed his arrest and ran naked from the guards, leaving his night clothes in the grasp of the soldier — an interesting and vivid detail likely to be remembered only by the person concerned. Like the famous film producer Alfred Hitchcock who always included himself in his films as an obscure bystander, Mark leaves us with a glimpse of himself innocently in the middle of the mighty deeds leading to Calvary.[15]

Dr Paul Barnett, lecturer in New Testament History at Macquarie University, Sydney, discusses the contribution of Peter in Mark's Gospel in his helpful book, *Is the New Testament History?* He concludes after carefully assembling the evidence: 'John Mark, then, was from a financially strong background, therefore educated and bilingual. He had been the close colleague of Barnabas, Paul and Peter and, by the time he was fifty years of age, had worked as a missionary with one or both of them for a decade and a half.'[16]

It is helpful to read *The Gospel according to Mark* underlining every passage where it says something about Peter. This gives a very interesting portrait of Peter in his own words. Mark tells us more of the failures of Peter than any of the other Gospels.

Peter openly told of his own weaknesses. Mark mentions Peter by name as being present on occasions when Matthew does not mention Peter's name. Mark includes Peter's weaknesses, but not praise for him, as though the old fisherman had added humility to his qualities. Mark's Semitic terms are explained and Greek words are given a Romanised form as they would if written for a Roman audience.

When Peter proclaimed the gospel to Cornelius and his family in Caesarea, he outlined five points which are repeated as five sections in Mark's Gospel, as if the Gospel is an expanded version of that sermon Peter would have given on many occasions. The breathtaking movement, the suddenness of the action, the evidence that only an eyewitness could have included as detail and the vividness of the emotions all support the possibility of Mark writing Peter's account.

The Gospel was written possibly in the late 50s or just after Peter's death. Probably Mark was with Peter up to the time of his death in Rome. In the persecutions that followed the Roman fire of AD 64, Mark's Gospel was surely an invaluable aid in helping the early Christians maintain their faith.

(b) The Epistles of Peter
The background of growing persecution is the scene against which *The First Epistle of Peter* was written close to the end of his life. Both epistles were written from Rome, called 'Babylon' in *Revelation*, where Rome is portrayed as the harlot Babylon dripping with the blood of the saints.

In some parts the persecution had already begun. In Pergamum, at the site of the great altar of Zeus, faithful Antipas was roasted to death for his witness to Jesus. Even acceptance of the name of Jesus was sufficient to warrant persecution.[17] These words of Peter on how Christians should react to persecution were to be their guiding lights until the peace which came in the East under the Toleration Edicts of Galerius in 311, and in the West in 313 under Constantine.

In the first epistle, Peter said the trials the Christians in Asia Minor would undergo would last only a limited time and that God would use them as a refiner's fire. Like Jesus, they would have to suffer for doing good. Such sufferings were part of Jesus' sufferings. In spite of the persecution, Christians must be obedient to the civil authorities even though greater suffering may come upon them.[18]

In the early church, persecution was at first localised. There is no evidence — Hollywood films notwithstanding — of widespread persecution under Nero outside of Rome. But after the murder of James in Jerusalem in AD 62, Christianity ceased to be regarded as a protected sect of Judaism. Subsequently, Christians were open to slander, defamation, mob violence and death.[19]

The Second Epistle of Peter was written to help Christians facing false teachers and so speaks of their destruction on the coming 'Day of the Lord'. The early believers were facing a world of immorality, insubordination, scepticism, the twisting of God's word and greed.[20]

A number of apocryphal works have also been attributed to Peter, but are most unlikely to be authentic. They were attributed to him by enthusiastic writers, although the early church was quick to deny them. *The Gospel of Peter* was clearly not authentic and, in AD 190, the church at Rhossus in Syria banned the writing because it had inaccuracies and a tendency to heresy. *The Apocalypse of Peter*, which relies on the schema of *The Revelation of John*, contains very colourful imaginings of the nature of hell. *The Acts of Peter* was likewise rejected as apocryphal for its fanciful filling-in of the details of the unknown journeys of Peter, complete with a description of his own martyrdom. However, these second century writings are important for the insights they give us into how Peter was regarded by the early church.

The Roman Forum

The Appian Way

The persecuted pastor

Somewhere near the end of his life, Peter went to Rome. He was not in Rome at the time Paul wrote *Romans*, but arrived some thirty years after the resurrection of Jesus, when he was about sixty-five.

In the year 64 Nero, in a fit of madness, tried to burn down the slum area of Rome to build a new city worthy of himself. The fire could not be controlled and many people were burnt to death. In the inquiry that followed, Nero blamed the Christians for starting the fire. As a result, many were brought to trial and put to death for their faith.

Some Christians rescued Peter and his wife so that he might continue his ministry of caring for

Left: The Roman Forum today

the remainder. Tradition states that as he turned his back upon the burning city of Rome where his brothers and sisters were suffering to take the message to another place, he had a vision of Jesus. Jesus looked at Peter and Peter said: 'Quo Vadis Dominie?' — 'Where are you going Lord?' And Jesus said, 'I am going to my people, Peter.' Peter suddenly realised he should not be turning his back on the people and, turning again, he went into the city of Rome.

Peter was taken prisoner and crucified. As they were about to nail him down, he protested that he was not worthy to die as Jesus had. With a mark of grim humour, his executioners nailed him on the cross upside down. So Peter died. This tradition is unanimous and strong in the early writers. Tacitus quotes it, Clement adds that it was at the same time as Paul was executed, Gaius dates it to Nero's persecution, Dionysius refers to his death as a martyrdom at the same time as Paul's, Sulpicius Servus speaks of the manner of the crucifixion, and Tertullian reports it.

He was buried, it is said, along the Via Appia where he had been walking alongside the body of the apostle Paul. The two great preachers of the early church were buried side by side. Eusebius refers to the monuments built to mark the place as 'trophies of the apostles', a traditional way of referring to the martyrs.

Christian leaders in Rome in the year AD 258 are said to have removed the bones of Paul and Peter, Paul's bones being laid at the church known as 'St Paul's Outside the Walls' on the Ostian Way, and Peter's eventually being laid at the site of a new church which the Emperor Constantine built, the basilica of St Peter.

This site, Vatican Hill, was originally Nero's gardens where, according to Tacitus, Christians were martyred. In AD 95 Clement, who was Bishop in Rome, wrote to the Corinthian Christians urging them to follow the brave faithfulness of Peter and Paul whom he knew personally, and whom he said were martyred in Rome. This is the first reference to them outside the New Testament. We do not know the exact site of the interred bones. Tradition said it was under the high altar of St Peter's, but in that greatest and largest of all churches, where several additions have been made, who could excavate underneath the high altar to make sure?

But in 1939, builders had to do some work on the foundations of the high altar in St Peter's at Rome. Archeologists found, in the debris underneath, two rows of mausoleums in which wealthy Romans had buried their families. Most of these are from the fourth century. One small mausoleum dating from the third century contains some Christian mosaics. On one wall is a Galilean fisherman, on another is Jonah being swallowed by a whale and on another a damaged mosaic perhaps representing the Good Shepherd. Nearby in a similar Christian tomb is a picture of an old man, carefully drawn in red lead and coloured in, featuring a bald head, furrowed brow and pointed beard. The name is Petrus — Peter. Beneath it is a prayer to the apostle requesting his intercession for all the Christians buried nearby.

Nearby is a memorial erected about AD 160 to Peter. Beneath that are the remains of earlier burials, perhaps as early as AD 70 and, in a cavity, the bones of a strong, tall, elderly man. As much as the church wanted to, Pope Pius XII stated it was impossible to identify these bones as those of Peter the Big Fisherman. Perhaps in the persecution, the body of Peter was not identified or preserved, but the place where he was martyred would have been identified. The site of St Peter's is probably the site of his death and maybe the memorial over his remains. One architectural piece of evidence is interesting: the original basilica built by Constantine was orientated around this early mausoleum.

A tombstone, written in
Latin, in the Catacombs, Rome

Peter's influence through the church of Rome

Peter had not founded the church in Rome, but his martyrdom there gave the church great prestige. As the chief city of the empire, the church there assumed a position of importance. The deaths of Peter and Paul gave strength to this assumption. Their deaths gave the church at Rome apostolic roots.

From AD 200, a devout cult grew up around both Peter and Paul. Constantine reinforced this by building over the site of Peter's martyrdom. By the time of Pope Leo the Great, who died in 461, Peter was claimed as the first bishop of Rome, and the direct antecedent of all subsequent popes, who could now trace their descent to Peter, the leader of the twelve disciples.

There is no New Testament evidence to link Peter with a chain of successive bishops of Rome or that Peter was bishop of Rome during the period AD 41 to 66. If Paul's sixteenth chapter of Romans was actually written to the Christians in Rome,[21] then it would be incredible that among all the people in the Roman church mentioned, Paul would omit to mention Peter, especially if Peter had been bishop. According to tradition Paul wrote the pastoral epistles to Timothy and Titus, yet he says that during his imprisonment in Rome 'only Luke is with me'.[22] Peter claimed that his mission was to be to the Jews and to the members of the lost ten tribes of Israel.[23] While these verses can be explained in various ways, the collective evidence seems to point to Peter being active among the Jews in Asia Minor rather than being bishop in Rome. However, this does not preclude Peter visiting Rome and dying there, concluding his last journey.

Having said this, we should be careful not to overlook the real significance of Peter in Rome and in the early church. It lies in his original confession of faith that Jesus was the Christ, in his leadership of the Twelve, in his witness to the resurrection, in his message of the gospel on the Day of Pentecost, in his missionary journeys, in *The Gospel of Mark* and his own epistles, and in the example of his faithfulness unto death. While Peter was neither the theologian nor the missionary strategist that Paul was, he was instrumental in the establishment of the church and its growth since.

Pope John Paul II greets pilgrims to St Peter's, Rome

For personal reading

Theme: Effective leader

MONDAY	Prison	*Acts 12:1-19*
TUESDAY	Opposition and defence	*Acts 11:1-18*
WEDNESDAY	Solution	*Acts 15:1-21*
THURSDAY	Cornerstone	*1 Peter 2:4-10*
FRIDAY	Duties	*1 Peter 2:11 — 4:11*
SATURDAY	Faithfulness	*1 Peter 5:1-11*
SUNDAY	Readiness	*1 Peter 4:12-19; 3:15b-19*

For group study

Topic: Faith and culture

1 Why was it necessary in the first century to resolve the problem of prospective believers becoming Jews before they could join the Christians?

2 What relevance does the issue of circumcision as it affected the young church have today?

3 Are there any rules and regulations that Christians should follow today?

4 How important is it that we know where Peter and Paul were buried?

5 What have you learned from the life of Peter?

4

Stephen the Martyr

Jerusalem, not Galilee or Samaria, was central to the Christian church immediately after Pentecost. This was despite the fact that Jesus and most of the disciples came from Galilee and a number of early Christians from Samaria. James and the Jerusalem church, who were strongly supportive of the Law and the Temple, were wary of those from areas of Palestine such as Galilee and Samaria where the Christians under greater Hellenic influence had less obvious respect for

Jewish traditions. Stephen was on a collision course with Jerusalem for, as will be shown, he appears to have been a Hellenic Samaritan Christian. To understand the conflict we need to understand Hellenism and Samaritans in the first century.

Hellenism in the first century
The Hellenists were those people, of whatever ethnic origin, who were convinced of the superiority of Greek culture, language and lifestyle, and who adopted it in preference to their indigenous culture, language and lifestyle. Following the conquest of Asia Minor by Alexander the Great, Greek culture, language and lifestyle influenced every nation in the Middle East. Alexander's successors and the Romans continued this process. The Romans, powerful in war, were overcome in ideology. Captive Greece took Rome captive from within.

The common Greek language was spoken everywhere, intermarriage with Greek colonists was frequent and Greek customs were considered cultured. The Greek practice of colonisation throughout the world meant that centres of Hellenism were established in most countries.

Under the Greeks, the Jews were granted great freedom to pursue culture and learning. The Jewish community at Alexandria in North Africa, for example, became particularly active in intellectual and cultural pursuits. But the enforced Hellenisation of the Jews in Palestine after the succession of the Seleucids in 198 BC led to Jewish resistance under the Maccabees for a couple of decades. Hellenistic influence, however, continued under the Romans down to the time of Jesus.

The spread of Jews about the Mediterranean from the time of the Babylonian exile meant they were separated over centuries from the ritual, the Temple and the intense tradition of their culture in Jerusalem. More than a hundred cities of the ancient world are known to have possessed large Jewish communities. A number of the cities were mentioned as the homes for the Jews listening to Peter on the Day of Pentecost.[1] The impact of this dispersion gradually weakened the influence of the Temple and the traditions found in Judea among those in far-off countries. Occasional visits to Jerusalem showed them a world markedly different from their own. Lacking the Temple, the centre of their life focused on the synagogue which became the place of worship, education, commerce, law and social activities. There was natural tension between the Aramaic-speaking, Temple-centred local Hebrews in Jerusalem and the Greek-speaking, synagogue-centred, Hellenic Jews from other countries.

In Alexandria, the influence of Hellenic culture was very strong. Jewish philosophers like Philo adopted Greek methods of interpretation, especially the allegorical method, and applied them to the Old Testament. This led to conflict with Orthodox Jews who believed sacred truth was

being intermingled with pagan philosophy. It was here the Old Testament was translated by seventy scholars into Greek. This translation, known as the Septuagint, made the Hebrew scriptures available to an international audience and became the basis of much discussion of Hebrew monotheism. Some early Christian evangelists used this widely in proclaiming Jesus as Messiah.

Other centres of Hellenic culture in which there were large Jewish populations were Miletus, Ephesus and Tarsus in Asia Minor; Seleucia, Tripolis and Antioch in Syria; and Philippi, Thessalonica and Corinth in Greece. Each of these cities became receptive to the spreading Christian faith. The Jews here were different in their culture, language and lifestyle to the Jews in Judea.

One notable and eloquent Hellenic Jew who became Christian was Apollos from Alexandria. He knew the Greek Old Testament well and used his fluency in Greek and his knowledge of the scriptures to argue that Jesus was the Messiah.

He had arrived in Corinth after Paul had established the church there and, after Paul had left, continued in leadership. His powerful expositions won many converts and some claimed to belong to his 'party'. Paul's first letter to the Corinthians argues against this party spirit. The way Paul speaks about Apollos[2] indicates he had good relationships with him, for he speaks more freely of him than he does about those who supported the party of Peter with whom he had face-to-face confrontation.

Apollos also visited Ephesus where his powerful preaching attracted much attention. Priscilla and Aquila spoke with him privately in their home about their better understanding of baptism and there, with great enthusiasm, he proclaimed and

taught correctly the facts about Jesus. With his strong arguments he defeated the Jews in public debates by proving from the scriptures that Jesus was the Messiah.[3] The term 'eloquent speaker' was frequently used to describe a person of Hellenic culture. Apollos was typical of the early Christians from Hellenic backgrounds. They became Christians in large numbers, probably outnumbering the Hebraic Jews who became Christians.

Hellenism has had an important impact on various parts of Palestine. In Judea it had little. The use of Aramaic as an everyday language, the proximity of the Temple, and the education system centred upon the synagogue and the teaching of the Torah mean that the Greek influence was limited.

The impact of Hellenism upon Galilee was far greater than any other territory in Palestine. This was partly due to the geography of the area which allowed easy access to foreigners with their different languages and customs. Through Galilee ran the great trade routes from the east to the west and from the north to the south, and its people were exposed to cosmopolitan influences more frequently than the cities in the Judean hills, including Jerusalem.

The Galileans were sneered at by orthodox Jews in Jerusalem as uncouth, with harsh guttural speech which betrayed them easily. The Galileans' openness to change meant that they responded to the greater freedom that Jesus spoke about in religious observance. Jesus, not surprisingly, was criticised by the Jews in the highlands of the south for allowing ceremonial laxity and lack of concern for tradition.

But there were many Greek towns in Palestine, not just in Galilee, which became centres of Hellenic influence, many of them with a majority of non-Jewish inhabitants. Caesarea had a Jewish community of 20,000 who were a minority in the city. The Roman amphitheatres and Temple to Augustus dominated the city. Other cities in the Decapolis region, such as Gadara, were all centres of non-Jewish culture, as were Ptolemais and Scythopolis.

South of Galilee, in Samaria, there was also constant dispute with the Jews of Jerusalem and the Hellenic Jews from Galilee. They had their own traditions that varied from those in Jerusalem and had also been influenced by Greek culture. There were some Christians among them. These Samaritan Christians played an important, though often unrecognised, part in the history of the first century church.

Left and below: Caesarea today

Stephen the Samaritan Christian
Dr Abram Spiro has argued cogently that Stephen was a Samaritan Christian.[4] He presents fourteen scholarly arguments to support his view. His views are compelling, indicating how Stephen reflects the Samaritan view of Old Testament history: the inferior place of Moses, the exaltation of Abraham and his use of the Samaritan version of the Law.[5]

The use of the Samaritan text variations was followed by Stephen in more than a score of instances, some of them very significant diversions. The Samaritan text features the addition of participles and prepositions designed to make for smoother reading, the inclusion of expansions sometimes several paragraphs in length to help elaborate or explain a point and Babylonian traditions which support Samaritan historical viewpoints. Some of these are mentioned by Stephen.[6]

For example, Stephen consistently quotes Abraham as leaving Harran upon his father's death[7] which is a Samaritan viewpoint of history which had old Terah living until he was 145 years of age. However, the Jews quoted from their Masoretic text, used by Christians, which indicates that Terah lived for 205 years, not dying until sixty years after Abraham left Harran.[8] Stephen quotes the words of Moses, 'I am the God of your fathers',[9] using the plural of the Samaritan text instead of the singular as was found in the Masoretic text. The Samaritans claimed Mt Gerizim and the nearby Shechem as the true place of worship and here a rival temple to that at Jerusalem was constructed. Stephen twice mentions Shechem and the tomb there owned by Abraham and their belief that Abraham was buried there and not, as the Jews believed, in Machpelah.[10]

This of course was an insult to the Jews and a key point of dispute. Shechem was the place where God appeared to Abraham, where he built an altar and, in their view, the correct place — 'holy place' — for a shrine.

Stephen went further in his address indicating that Solomon's Temple was not only in the wrong place, but was of human origin. When Stephen quoted the scriptures: 'What kind of house would you build for me? Where is the place for me to live in? Did not I myself make all these things?'[11] he was quoting from the Samaritan source which makes three questions and changes the context of the Jewish text. Even the quoting of these changed verses would have brought the ire of the Jews upon him.

A further insight into Stephen's Samaritan background is the way he quotes God dealing personally with Abraham, whereas he claims God dealt with Moses only through an angel in the giving of the Law.[12] This shows the superiority of Abraham over Moses, but it is in direct conflict with the Jewish tradition.[13]

There is strong evidence, therefore, for Stephen's Samaritan origin.

The tensions between Jews and Samaritans had strong historical and theological roots, and the Christians who developed in both communities shared the difference of traditions and theologies, including their knowledge of the scriptures. The Jewish hatred of the Samaritans is illustrated in many parts of the New Testament. Jesus spoke against it with telling effect in his famous parable of the good Samaritan.[14] To most, this was a contradiction in terms, for Samaritans were thought of in terms of traitors and heretics.

Electing the first deacons

The Samaritans were the only people for centuries to call themselves 'Hebrews'. The Jews of the first century were never called Hebrews, neither did they describe themselves as Hebrews, and it was only in the second century that the Jews were referred to by this term. The 'Hebrews' in Acts 6:1, therefore, are clearly Samaritan Christians, a minority group among the Christians — as were the Hellenic Jewish Christians. It was these two groups that argued about the neglect of their widows in the daily food distribution. The tension over this issue in the early church necessitated the appointment of some additional church officers to oversee the caring and administrative functions of the church. In the dispute over the administration of relief, and in the answer of the appointment of the deacons, the Jerusalem Christians and the apostles, who were in Jerusalem, took no part. To the Jewish Christians, both the Samaritan and the Hellenic Christians were people who had deviated from the orthodox Jewish traditions. This issue over the administration of relief was a dispute between the two minority groups.

The seven chosen deacons were thought to be full of the Holy Spirit and wisdom and were well equipped to set about their task of administering social relief. They were certainly not just 'table waiters' as their title suggests, for they also started preaching and evangelising. Without delay Stephen moved throughout the Hellenic synagogues preaching the Lordship of Jesus with powerful effect. Up to now, the main activity of the gospel lay in the apostles proclaiming in the Temple. Now Stephen was disputing in the synagogues. The locus of proclamation had changed for all time, and thereafter Paul and others would find the synagogue the centre of their debate and proclamation.

His preaching in the Hellenic synagogues was to cause much strife, a charge before the Jewish Sanhedrin and his death. Stephen no sooner enters church history than he leaves it, but not without having profound effect. He would declare that the new had come, therefore the old must go; the Sanhedrin declared the old must stay, therefore the new must go.

Stephen before the Sanhedrin

The report of Stephen's defence is one of the longest speeches in the whole Bible, is the longest in Acts and is even longer than the three sermons of Paul put together. He outlines the history of the Jewish race and quotes many Old Testament passages in support of his argument. As indicated earlier, he relied very much on the Samaritan text. Further, he mentions that favourite word of Hellenic philosophy, wisdom, four times, even though it is nowhere else mentioned in Acts.

Stephen's powerful witness created a backlash. Many today

Cardinal Joseph Mindszenty — tried and convicted by the Budapest People's Court, 1949

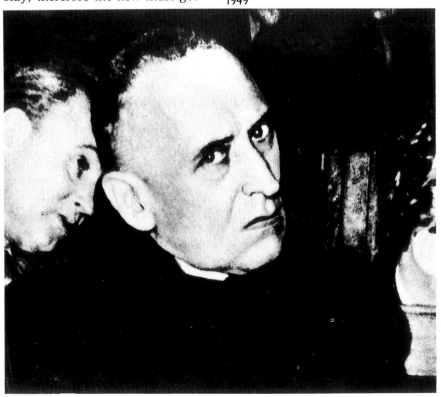

The outside wall of the Temple area

have misunderstood the reasons for which Stephen was condemned. None of the reasons was distinctively part of the Christian gospel, but reflect the conflict between the Hellenic Jews and the Samaritan Christians.

It was the Hellenic members of the synagogues of the Freedmen, which included Jews from Alexandria, Cyrene, Cilicia and Asia Minor, who instigated complaints against Stephen's preaching in their midst on the grounds that 'we have heard him speaking against Moses and God'.[15] Now this is obviously not part of the gospel, but it was part of the Samaritan-Jewish conflict. Stephen's detractors thought he elevated the role of Abraham and denigrated the role of Moses. Furthermore, Stephen was charged with speaking firstly against the Temple in Jerusalem — an echo, surely, of the Samaritan woman talking to Jesus about Mt Gerizim being the proper place to worship God instead of the Temple in Jerusalem — and secondly against the Law of Moses. These were typical charges against Samaritan teaching. Only the reference to Jesus destroying the Temple has any Christian content.[16]

His speech which occupies most of Acts 7 is carefully constructed. We will not examine the speech in detail here except to say that Stephen neither defends himself against the charge, nor does he proclaim the gospel as did Peter and John. In fact, the name of Jesus Christ is not mentioned. He was perhaps cut short before he came to proclaiming the life, death and resurrection of Jesus. Instead, he concentrates on the Law and the Temple and how his listeners have resisted the Holy Spirit and murdered the righteous servant of God.

Stephen was possibly the first to realise the temporal nature of the Law, the Temple and the ritual that surrounded it. His criticism of the Temple and the attitudes that followed from the way the Temple was promoted was also made by others, in a less radical form, at the time.

The Essene community at Qumran, for example, was critical of the high priesthood whom they claimed was illegitimate and needed to be replaced by the true high priestly line from Zadok, and critical, too, of the whole worship cult centring on the Temple. They awaited the Messianic age when they would return to Jerusalem and restore the Temple and the high

priesthood to its true worship and legitimacy. Oscar Cullmann has suggested that from the Qumran community were some of the 'great number of priests who accepted the faith'.[17]

All that was central to the life of the Jews was now fulfilled and focused in Jesus Christ. In this insight was the seeds of the equality of Jew and Gentile within the church and the end of the unique place of Judaism. Little wonder the Jerusalem Jews, and even other Hellenic Jews, felt him to be a traitor and his teaching heretical. Death had to follow. Stephen had first criticised the institutions and the Temple in the Synagogue of the Freedmen, which had resulted in a great deal of argument there. The Hellenists, with their love for logic, were the first to see the implications of Stephen's preaching. It is to be doubted that even the apostles had followed through the logic of it. Paul understood: that is why he approved of Stephen's murder.

Whether Stephen's address was a frequently used formula or not we don't know, but certainly the early church developed the theme used here of the people of God becoming the divine dwelling-place and Paul, Peter, John and the author of *The Letter to the Hebrews* all wrote on that subject.

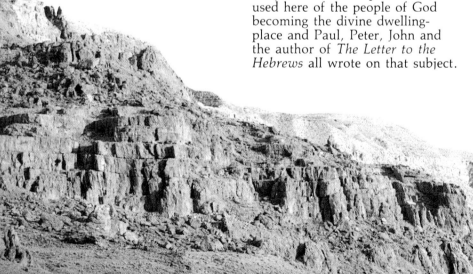

Stephen's martyrdom

Stephen was the first Christian to lay down his life for his faith. He became the important historical and theological link between Peter and Paul, between the church of the Jews and the church of the Gentiles, between the church in Judea and the church of the uttermost parts of the world. Cameos of his death that have survived from the days of the young church testify to the importance of this event.

When the Council members became furious, gnashing their teeth, rushing upon him, in anger striking him, Stephen calmly looked at the open heavens and saw the ascended Jesus by the side of God. He was thrown outside the city walls and stoned to death. As they continued to stone him, he knelt and, like the Lord Jesus, prayed for his tormentors' forgiveness and entrusted himself into the hands of Jesus.

The scene was probably more violent than that. He was probably thrown down from a twenty metre high wall and large boulders dropped upon his kneeling then prostrate body.

Stephen was not put to death solely because of his proclamation of the Christian gospel, but partly because, being a Samaritan Christian, he infuriated the Jews and the Hellenists by rejecting their Law, their Temple, Moses, and their Mosaic customs and by spreading Samaritan concepts.

The result of this martyrdom was that 'all believers, except the apostles, were scattered throughout the provinces of Judea and Samaria'.[18]

Some of the believers who were scattered by the persecution which took place when Stephen was killed, went as far as Phoenicia, Cyprus and Antioch, telling the message to Jews only. But other believers, men from Cyprus and Cyrene, went to Antioch and proclaimed the message to Gentiles also, telling them the good news about the Lord Jesus.[19]

The result was that the church in Jerusalem became more conservative and, with the majority of the Hellenists forced to flee, much more Hebrew in its composition. Ironically, their leader James, who attended the Temple daily and was known for his devotion in prayer and the Law, was himself eventually brought before the Sanhedrin and also executed by stoning like Stephen.

Stephen's influence on Paul

Stephen's lasting impact, however, was in the effect the manner of his death had upon Saul of Tarsus. Saul watched with approval. That approval, a consent that is deliberately written into the account, burned itself deep into Saul's mind and decades later he remembered: 'when Stephen was put to death, I myself was there, approving of his murder and taking care of the cloaks of his murderers.'[20]

In the death of this Samaritan Christian who spoke against the Jewish heritage he held so dear, Saul saw a man dying in faith. His own confidence in the ritual of the Temple and the traditions of the Jerusalem Jews was shaken. Saul's conversion experience, which was to culminate on the Damascus Road, began at that point. As Augustine said centuries later: 'If Stephen had not prayed, the church would not have had Paul.'[21]

As a native of Cilicia, Paul may have been one of the Cilician members of the synagogue of the Freedmen who had charged Stephen before the Council of the Sanhedrin which meant that, as an accuser, he was required by law to be present at his execution. Certainly, in the persecution of Christians that broke out just after, Paul took a leading part and, as he said, 'I was devoted to the Jewish religion and I persecuted without mercy the church of God and did my best to destroy it.'[22]

The impact of the brief ministry of Stephen is seen in his importance as a bridge between the ministries of Peter and Paul, an example of the ministries of Samaritan Christians who first faced persecution for their faith, and as a noble witness to Jesus in his preaching, his trials and his death. Although brief, his ministry was crucial in the history of the young church.

For personal reading

Theme: The first martyr

MONDAY
A need
Acts 6:1-7

TUESDAY
Arrest
Acts 6:8-15

WEDNESDAY
Defence 1
Acts 7:1-29

THURSDAY
Defence 2
Acts 7:30-53

FRIDAY
Death
Acts 7:54 — 8:3

SATURDAY
Results 1
Acts 9:1-22

SUNDAY
Results 2
Acts 22:3-21

For group study

Topic: Faith and tradition

1   Why did some Jews not like the influences of Greek culture on their religion?

2   How are we able to distinguish the cultural aspects of our faith from the heart of the gospel?

3   How can we avoid the danger of following tradition rather than the word of God?

4   What was there about Stephen's speech before he died that made Saul start to think about his new faith (Acts 7:1-53)?

5   What can Stephen teach Christians today?

5

James and Jude

In the city of Sydney there are many people in desperate need who really need care. Henry Lawson, the Australian poet, looking from an office window summed up the situation in this way:

And cause I have to sorrow,
in a land so young and fair
to see upon these faces
stamped the marks of want and care.
I look in vain for traces
of fresh and fair and sweet
in the sallow sunken faces
that go drifting in the street.

Wesley Central Mission, in the centre of Sydney, is one agency that has sought to both worship

God and meet these needs. It provides for worship and service to the poor, the unemployed, the homeless, the aged, the drug addict, the orphan and many other needy in the community.

Similarly, the early church was a church that knew how to go out in practical service to people in need. Its members cared for the widows in need. They looked after little children. Orphans were mentioned specifically in the New Testament. They cared for people who were hungry. They gave property, offerings, food and clothing to those who had special needs. Theirs was a practical faith that went up to God in expressions of worship and that went out in care for people right in the heart of their cities.

James, the brother of Jesus
One man who particularly stressed the practical nature of faith was James. He wrote to the young church to encourage people not just to believe but also to serve.

This is not the disciple James who was the son of Zebedee; he is not the other disciple James who was the son of Alphaeus; he is not the James who was the father of Judas (not Iscariot); but he was probably James the natural brother of Jesus.

Jude describes himself as a servant of Jesus Christ and brother of James.[1] He may have been a brother of Jesus: such a brother is named.[2] We know nothing about Jude's ministry and his letter is too general to give us details about where it was written or to whom it was written.

(a) The brother
The other children were always with Mary as a natural family would be.[3] The family did not believe that Jesus was God's Son at first and they did not follow him.[4] However, the elder brother James witnessed the resurrected Jesus and that changed his whole life.[5] He became a leader in the church particularly in Jerusalem.[6]

Each of the Gospels mentions James as the first of our Jesus' brothers and presumably the eldest. These younger men are described as our Lord's brothers, an interesting word that describes the special relationship these other members of the family of Jesus had with him and which promoted them into the leadership of the early church after they came to faith.[7]

Many do not accept that these are brothers of Jesus in the natural sense, but are only 'cousins' — and the word 'brother' while usually used in the normal sense can occasionally refer to a cousin or a member of the same clan or fellowship group. Others describe them as 'half brothers', children of Joseph by a previous marriage. St Jerome, in AD 383, developed a doctrine supporting the perpetual virginity of Mary. To him it was important that Mary had no more children. So these previously-mentioned brothers were treated as cousins.

But Matthew says clearly:

Jesus taught in the synagogue and those who heard him were amazed. 'Where did he get such wisdom?' they asked. 'And what about his miracles? Isn't he the carpenter's son? Isn't Mary his mother? And aren't James, Joseph, Simon and Judas his brothers? Aren't all his sisters living here? Where did he get all this?' And so they rejected him.[8]

We know something about this James. While Jesus was working in Nazareth as a carpenter, James decided to study for the priesthood. He went away to Jerusalem and learnt all the intricacies of the Old Testament and the Jewish faith. An ancient tradition has it that he used to spend long hours in prayer, so long, in fact, that the skin on his knees became really calloused from kneeling down for so many hours every day, giving rise to an early nickname: 'Camel Knees'.

(b) The church leader

The training James received as a priest meant that the young church had within its key leadership someone with professional training and education.

The other apostles — Peter, Matthew, John, Philip, Andrew and others — went to different parts of the world preaching the gospel as overseas missionaries. Someone had to stay at home and care for the young church, and that was James the brother of Jesus. Clement of Alexandria, an early church leader, indicates that James was chosen for the leadership of the church in Jerusalem by Peter and John and Jerome states that he was chosen by the apostles as the first bishop of Jerusalem.

James was a traditional Jew. He wore the phylactries around his head and bound them on his forearm. He wore a prayer shawl over his head and shoulders. The early Christian writers indicate that he was conservative and not too keen on the gospel being taken to the Gentiles. Only through the argument of Paul and Peter was he eventually convinced. He had a concern about the question of circumcision and he was the chairman of the Council of Jerusalem which discussed the question of circumcising the Gentiles.

This young Jewish boy is shown being received into the Jewish faith.

Stoning usually took place outside the city wall and was carried out by paid executioners.

(c) The martyr

James was stoned to death in AD 62. There was conflict between the Christian leaders and the Jewish leaders at the instigation of the High Priest Ananius, son of Annas, who took part in the trial of Jesus.

The Roman procurator Festus had died and during the time before the arrival of the new procurator, Albinus, the opportunity was taken to get rid of some of the leaders of the early church. King Agrippa II, however, believed this would cause trouble with the new procurator and deposed Ananius.

The death of James caused many Christians in Jerusalem to be afraid and many fled to Pella, Egypt and the area around Ephesus.

(d) The author

Some scholars have accepted the Epistle of James as being written by others and named in honour of James, but everything in the epistle is consistent with what we know of James, and his early training and scholarship certainly prepared him for his leadership task and for writing the epistle. As he did not travel like Paul, a general letter such as we have would be expected.

The form of the letter is quite distinct from that of other New Testament letters, expecially those of Paul. There is no situational immediacy for the writing of the letter. It is similar to other first century exhortatory letters and to the book of Proverbs.

The teaching of James

This letter was probably a written sermon that James had preached on many occasions, covering the manner in which the Christians should live within the Jewish cultural environment. There is little in it that an orthodox Jew could not accept. There are many points of close connection with Jesus' Sermon on the Mount.[9] There are some parallels with other early Christian writings like 1 Peter, Clement of Rome's Letter to the Corinthian Church, and the Shepherd of Hermas.

The letter was always highly valued but in every conference of the church concerning the content of the New Testament canon, the place of James was questioned. This was not because of problems over authorship, but because of the practical teaching of James which seemed to come into conflict with Paul's teaching on the essential nature of faith. It is, however, an apparent, not a real contradiction. James insists on works of the Jewish Law that have to do with our faith expressed in action in compassionate service to others. The works of the Law that Paul condemns are those ritualistic requirements that people substituted instead of trust in God's unconditional acceptance of us. James seems to be aware of Paul's teaching, and seems to correct those who misused Paul's emphasis upon the faith that saves by neglecting our obligations to serve.

The letter was written in Greek as can be seen from the clever wordplays.[10] But there are many semitisms that arise from the Hebrew scriptures rather than from the Greek translation of the Old Testament, the Septuagint, which is consistent with a man trained as a priest, learning the scriptures in Hebrew. The Jewishness in this letter is more marked than that of any other book in the New Testament except the epistles of John.

James was a great man of faith and his faith was a practical faith. He speaks about testing, wisdom, wealth, speech, envy, patience, prayer and neighbourly conduct and, having mentioned each of these aspects in the first chapter, develops each of them in the later chapters.

His main concern is that our faith must be expressed in our social obligations. We must not be hearers of the word only, but we must put it into practice (1:22). The royal law of God must be expressed as compassion for our neighbour. Ritual religion must develop into a religion that cares for the widow, the orphan and the helpless (1:26-27); refuses

Practical Christianity is about love in action

to show partiality (2:1-13); demonstrates compassion for the poor (2:14-26); has guarded speech (4:11-12); and demonstrates patience, prayer and faithful concern for the wayward (5:7-20).

James makes two major points: First, faith must be expressed in caring. Faith is not merely a matter of an intellectual understanding of God: it must also mean caring for other people. James puts it bluntly:

Does anyone think he is religious? If he does not control his tongue, his religion is worthless and he deceives himself. What God the Father considers is pure and genuine religion is this: to take care of orphans and widows in their suffering and to keep oneself from being corrupted by the world.[11]

Second, faith must be expressed in actions. It is not enough just to believe; faith must be put into practice in a practical way. James says:

My brothers, what good is it for someone to say that he has faith if his actions do not prove it? Can that faith save him? Suppose there are brothers and sisters who need clothes, and don't have enough to eat. What good is there in your saying to them 'God bless you! Keep warm and eat well!' — if you don't give them the necessities of life? So it is with faith: if it is alone and includes no actions, then it is dead.[12]

James points to two well-known people in Jewish history, Abraham and Rahab. Abraham put his faith into action when he left his home and country, went to a strange place under God's

leading and established a nation against all possible odds. Rahab was a prostitute condemned by the Law who gave shelter and protection to two Jewish spies, thus saving their lives and leading to the nation's successful capture of Jericho. Both of them cared and exercised their faith in action. 'So then, as the body without the spirit is dead, so also faith without actions is dead.'[13]

The Epistle of Jude

The epistle of Jude is one of the briefest in the Bible, containing only twenty-five verses. It is a general letter designed to encourage faithfulness against false teachers. It is a very Jewish piece of writing, drawing upon Old Testament and apocryphal imagery of Egypt, angels, Sodom and Gomorrah, the archangel Michael, Cain, Balaam and Korah, together with pastoral ideas from Zechariah and Enoch.

This little book is a small tract addressed to the believers encouraging them 'to fight on for the faith which once and for all God had given for his people'.[14]

From the earliest days it was accepted as authoritative, from the youngest brother of Jesus. The only doubts were raised because of his quoting from two of the apocryphal books of the Old Testament. Some scholars have pointed out the use of words was typical of a Galilean, and the words were very similar to those of James.

Jude's writing so closely parallels that of 2 Peter chapter 2 that they seem either to be dependent upon some common source or one has been dependent upon the other.

The challenge of practical faith

Let me root it finally right down in your heart. Is that your kind of faith? Because what good is it if you just talk words and not do deeds? Mother Teresa put it beautifully when she said: 'We have hearts to love and hands to serve.'

God is not just a talker; God is a doer. He not only gives words, but he does things. Jesus is not just a preacher. He went about preaching the gospel, but also he went about doing good. The church is not just a group of people that have beliefs; it is a family of servants who are willing to help.

A food line in Bangladesh

For personal reading

For group study

Topic: A brother remembers

1 Why didn't Jesus' brothers believe he was the Messiah?

2 How did James' early training equip him for the role of leader of the Jerusalem church?

3 How is James' writing different from that of many other New Testament writers?

4 What is the value of James' epistle today?

5 How is the message of Jude's letter still relevant today?

6

Timothy and Titus

From the beginning of history the central area of Turkey has seen villages and towns come and go. The remains of some ancient cities and towns are still visible, but some places which were once quite large towns have left no remains. The cities of Lystra, Derbe and Iconium were once quite large Roman outposts in the southern central region of Turkey. The mileposts along the highways have survived, but little of the towns themselves. They held defensive positions close to the mountains and, judging from the large number of Latin inscriptions found by archeologists in this area, must have held very large numbers of Roman soldiers.

Today, nothing remains. Likewise, the whole area of the churches to which Paul's Letter to the Galatians was sent is unknown to us, with scholars arguing for both northern or southern regions as the likely areas.

During the seventeen silent years after he had become a Christian and before he left on his first missionary journey, Paul visited this central area of Turkey regularly from his home town of Tarsus. When Paul and Barnabas left on their first missionary journey, it was only natural that they should come back to this area which Paul had visited some years before.

It was in the area of Derbe that Timothy first met Paul and became a Christian. Nearby Paul also met Titus and these two young men, both in their early twenties, continued on the missionary journey with Paul and became two of the first pastors of the early church.

Paul used these fit and enthusiastic young men in various ways: as evangelists, going into the surrounding areas to preach the gospel whenever he came into a major town; as pastors, to help the newly founded churches grow until elders and other leaders were appointed; as messengers, to carry the letters that Paul wrote to the churches that we now have in our New Testament; and as trouble-shooters, to help solve some of the problems in new congregations.

Paul trained a number of young men as pastors and evangelists to help the believers grow in the churches he established throughout the Roman world. There were Silas and John Mark, Demas and Crescens, Sopater of Berea, Aristarchus and Secundus from Thessalonica, Gaius, Titus and Timothy who came from the area of Derbe and Lystra, and Tychicus and Trophimus who came from Colossae.

Several of these young men travelled with Paul and he would leave one or more behind to pastor new churches recently established. Timothy was to go to Thessalonica, to Corinth, to Philippi and to Ephesus, while Titus was to be sent to Corinth, to Crete, to Nicopolis and to Dalmatia, now called Yugoslavia — although tradition in Albania also claims Titus as their first bishop.

Titus

We know little about the family life of Titus. He first appears when he travels with Barnabas and Paul to Jerusalem. Titus was a Gentile and not circumcised and some of the Jewish Christians were scandalised by this. They insisted that Titus be circumcised, but Paul refused, explaining to Titus that 'in order to keep the truth of the gospel safe for you, we did not give in to them for a minute'.[1]

Titus was the first Gentile pastor of the Christian church. He was an associate with Paul in the long ministry in Ephesus and took the first letter to the church in Corinth. He probably also took the missing second letter to Corinth as well, referred to as 'the severe letter'.

Part of his ministry was to correct particular church situations and to work in the difficult city of Corinth. The church was wracked by internal divisions and unworthy behaviour, while others had disputed Paul's leadership and authority. Titus was sent to correct this situation and travelled to Troas to meet up with Paul, who continued to move throughout Turkey.

When Paul arrived in Troas, Titus was not there to meet him which increased his anxiety about the younger man. But then, when Paul had crossed over to Macedonia, he met with Titus who was on his way to meet him. Titus reported the situation to Paul, relieving Paul's concern.

Paul immediately sent Titus back to Corinth to build the believers up in their faith and to make arrangements for the special

Corinth

offering that was required for the poor in Jerusalem. Paul complimented Titus by telling the Corinthians that they could judge Paul himself by the character of Titus.[2] Titus seems to have been a faithful and reliable servant.

Timothy

Timothy came from a mixed marriage. His mother, Eunice, was a Jew and his father was a Greek. That mixed marriage gave Timothy an insight into both cultures.

His Greek cultural background was to help Timothy when he went and ministered in the Greek cities of Corinth, Nicopolis, Thessalonica and Philippi. His mother's strong faith, firstly as a Jew and then as a Christian, was something for which Paul was thankful. He said, 'I remember the sincere faith you have, the kind of faith that your grandmother Lois and your mother Eunice also had. I am sure that you have it also.'[3]

Paul had visited this area during his seventeen silent years of ministry in Tarsus and it was during one of these visits that Timothy, his mother and grandmother had become Christians.

Paul opens four of his letters by associating the greetings from Timothy as well as from himself. In four of the letters he is specifically mentioned as a fellow worker of Paul's, and in five places in the Acts of the Apostles, Luke describes the labours of Timothy. Two of the pastoral letters are addressed to him.

Throughout his life, the picture of Timothy is one of a hard-working and faithful pastor who travelled widely to a number of the churches, counselling and guiding their spiritual growth, and becoming the leader of the second generation of Christian leaders. He was an example for other younger missionaries and pastors and, in such a capacity, the pastoral letters from Paul to him and Titus may have been typical rather than personal.

The pastoral epistles

The traditional view of the authorship of the pastoral letters is that, in about AD 64, just before his own death, Paul, with the help of his writer Luke, wrote two letters to Timothy and one to Titus.

These letters are full of advice to the young ministers on how to handle believers and situations that arise in church life. Their main aim is to confirm the believers in their faith, to establish a system of local church leadership and to build up 'the church of the living God, the pillar and support of the truth.'4 Paul has described them as fellow workers, labourers, ministers, servants, ambassadors of the gospel and so on. Paul says, 'He (Timothy) is the only one who shares my feelings and really cares about you... he has proved his worth and he and I, like a son and his father, have worked together for the sake of the gospel.'5

There are a number of difficulties with this viewpoint. For one thing, neither Timothy nor Titus were at this time as inexperienced and incompetent as the advice given to them makes them appear. They both were experienced and able missionaries and ministers. Some scholars believe that in these three letters we have large portions of letters written by Paul but gathered together and written in a more general form by Luke after Paul's death in such a way as to encourage any young minister. A number of recent scholars have taken this position.

The concepts of church government and the role of bishops or elders seems to date from a later period in the church's life, as do the warnings against heresy and the urgency for preventive measures in the church's life.

The writer perhaps believed Paul's advice and teaching was standard and authoritative and would be helpful to the younger men who were the successors of Timothy and Titus — in other words, the first professional clergy in the church. The issues fit the post-apostolic era and are similar in detail to other contemporary writings like *The Didache* and the *Letters of Ignatius*.

The author believes that the pastoral epistles include letters written by Paul and edited for later and wider distribution. For the sake of brevity, we will include these pastoral epistles with the other letters of Paul and refer to him as their author.

Missionary travels

Timothy and Titus travelled a great deal around the Mediterranean area in helping the young churches cope with problems and grow in their faith.

Timothy came to Corinth at least twice. Paul had sent him because the church was facing a number of problems among the members. The Corinthian church was surrounded by the immorality of the cult of Aphrodite, the goddess of love, and many of the members of the church had previously been followers of the Greek god. Over 500,000 people populated this important trading and commercial centre.

On the top of Acro-Corinth, a 1,875-foot-high-mountain overlooking the city, was built a fort and temple to Aphrodite, popularly known as the goddess of love. The temple was serviced by one thousand prostitutes.

The whole area became a centre for visiting sailors whose ships were being dragged over the *droklos*, or ship-slipway of rolling logs that covered the four-mile Corinthian isthmus. Ships were dragged overland to avoid the long voyage round the Peloponnesus.

Timothy had experience in working with Greeks and the lessons he had learnt from his Greek father certainly helped him. Some significant people in Corinth became members of the church, including Priscilla and Aquila and the city treasurer, Erastus.

Archeologists have discovered near the theatre a marble plaque set up when the new road had been completed with the following inscription: *Erastvs pro aedilitate S P Stravit* ('Erastus, in return for his aedileship, laid this pavement at his own expense'). The aedileship was a government post such as 'minister of public roads'. Is this the same Erastus, treasurer of the city, of whom Paul writes: 'My host Gaius, in whose house the church meets, sends you his greetings; Erastus, the city treasurer, and our brother Quartus send you their greetings'?[6]

Timothy was also with Paul when the church was first founded in Philippi far to the north and Paul sent him back there on a later occasion. In that letter, Paul said:

Corinth

Athens

I hope that I will be able to send Timothy to you soon, so that I may be encouraged by news about you. He is the only one who shares my feelings and who really cares about you. Everyone else is concerned only with his own affairs, not with the cause of Jesus Christ. And you yourselves know how he has proved his worth, how he and I, like a son and his father, have worked together for the sake of the gospel. So I hope to send him to you as soon as I know how things are going to turn out for me. And I trust in the Lord that I myself will be able to come to you soon.[7]

After Paul had established the church in Berea, he left Timothy behind to consolidate the work there. Timothy later caught up with Paul in Athens, gave him news of the churches far in the north, and was sent back by Paul to help the church at Thessalonica. From there he returned to share with Paul in Corinth. They laboured together for more than eighteen months. Archeologists discovered an inscription to the proconsul Gallio, mentioned by Paul, which dates their time here in Corinth to the years AD 51 and 52.

Then the time came for Timothy to be sent back to Thessalonica to help the church solve their misunderstanding of the second coming of Jesus. Paul sent his first letter to the Thessalonians with Timothy.

Some time later Timothy was back in Corinth helping minister to the church when Titus arrived from Ephesus, bearing a letter to the church at Corinth. Titus later took news back to Paul at

Ephesus telling him of the ministry of Timothy, and Paul sent a further two letters back with Titus to Corinth. A few years later Timothy was still ministering in this area, for when Paul revisited Corinth and wrote from there the letter to the Romans, he mentions the ministry that Timothy is conducting.

Paul wrote the two letters to Timothy while Timothy was ministering in the city of Ephesus in Turkey. Paul had spent three years establishing the church there and had a particular interest in the people. The lack of significant personal greetings in the pastoral letters to people in the local church is another reason for believing these pastoral letters only contain portions of Paul's original letters and were collated by a later hand for general use among younger ministers.

Ephesus was regarded as the principal city in Asia Minor, having some 300,000 inhabitants in the first century. It was the centre of the worship of Artemis or Diana, and the great temple here was the largest building in the world — three times larger than the Athenian Parthenon. There were also three huge temples to Caesar and a 25,500 seat theatre. Ephesus was also the international banking capital of the Roman world.

Priscilla and Aquila were here as leaders in the church when Paul asked Timothy to minister in what was to be one of the most important congregations in the first century.

Titus also served with him when Paul left to go back to Jerusalem. Paul was to be taken on to Rome and to be imprisoned there in about AD 63. It would have been at this time that Paul wrote the two letters to Timothy and one to Titus. The content of these three letters is very similar even though their structure is not close-knit. Paul made three main points: there should be right doctrine, good leadership and the scriptures should be taught.

Right doctrine

Paul told the young pastors to make sure they taught the right doctrine. They needed to turn people from false beliefs and to keep them in the truth:

I want you to stay in Ephesus, just as I urged you when I was on my way to Macedonia. Some people there are teaching false doctrines, and you must order them to stop. Tell them to give up those legends and those long lists of ancestors, which only produce arguments; they do not serve God's plan, which is known by faith. The purpose of this order is to arouse the love that comes from a pure heart, a clear conscience and a genuine faith.

Some people have turned away from these and have lost their way in foolish discussions. They want to be teachers of God's law, but they do not understand their own words or the matters about which they speak with so much confidence.[8]

Paul wanted to build a church based upon pure love, a clear conscience and a genuine faith. He wanted Timothy to make sure that people would keep clear of false teaching: 'The Spirit says clearly that some people will abandon the faith in later times; they will obey lying spirits and follow the teaching of demons. Such teachings are spread by deceitful liars, whose consciences are dead, as if burnt by a hot iron.'[9]

Instead, he urged Timothy to teach the right doctrine and preach that Jesus Christ is Lord, and not be afraid of the fact that he was only a young man. 'Give them these instructions and these teachings. Do not let anyone look down on you because you are young, but be an example for the believers in your speech, your conduct, your love, faith and purity.'[10]

The false teaching encountered by the young pastors was causing great harm in the church. But others had faced a similar problem. The writers of the letters of Jude, 2 Peter, 1 John and the Revelation of John refer to it. Paul faced problems from Jewish Christians who insisted that true believers should fulfil all the requirements of the Jewish religion to be complete Christians. Paul argues strongly in Romans, Galatians and Ephesians that we are no longer under the imprisoning reign of the Jewish Law, but that we live in the realm of God's grace and the Spirit's freedom.

In the pastoral epistles, the young church was facing another problem from people who were influencing the believers. These believers, generally converts from Judaism, believed they were above the Law and were no longer subject to God's moral commands. They had a superior knowledge or *gnosis* that made them different from others and superior in their rights.

In reply, Paul argued that the Law is good if it keeps us from wrongdoing, and to this end the scriptures are given for 'rebuking error, correcting faults, and giving instruction for right living.'[11] Christians were not people who opposed the Law; they obeyed it, yet did not live their lives in bondage to it. Christians kept a delicate balance: by living out the indwelling life of Christ, they live in accordance with the Law's demands, not by obeying rules, but by being close followers of Jesus who fulfilled the Law.

The gnostic philosophy was to become a major heresy in the second century of the church's history. But already it was developing a system of 'legends and long lists of ancestors', 'godless legends which are not worth telling', and 'Jewish legends and human commandments which come from people who have rejected the truth.'[12] They were to come to believe their superior spirituality would remove them from the evil of all matter. They would completely renounce this world, and the flesh would be mortified.

Ephesus

Good leaders

Timothy was urged to appoint church members who would be good leaders in the work. Good leaders would insist on right doctrine and correct the wrong emphasis of the false teachers and leaders. Both 1 Timothy and Titus reject leaders whose 'minds do not function and who no longer have the truth. They think that religion is a way to become rich.'[13] How every generation needs to be on guard against such bad examples of leadership!

The pastoral epistles to Timothy and Titus show us Paul encouraging both these young men to appoint bishops or elders and deacons in their church. It was obvious by this time that Titus was being regarded as a travelling bishop and Timothy as a settled bishop and the early church was moving to appointing church leaders who had the responsibility for oversight of the local congregation.

These epistles reveal the growing stages of the early church's government, and consequently cannot be used to provide a blueprint for contemporary church government. Side by side, we have the germinating seeds of what one group of Christians see as an episcopal system of church government, another sees as a presbyterian form of church government, and others see as a congregational form of church government. The fact is that the pastoral epistles do not contain any developed form of government, but simply general instructions in the selection of right leaders to meet the needs of a young church facing a severe test at the point of its doctrine and leadership.

Both Timothy and Titus had the qualifications that were necessary for such positions. Paul said, 'if a man is eager to be a church leader he desires an excellent work' and he outlined the role of bishops or elders and deacons, stressing that they had to be mature Christian characters so as to produce maturity in others. As Paul says, Timothy's task was to 'be strong through the grace that is ours in union with Christ Jesus. Take the teachings that you heard me proclaim in the presence of many witnesses, and entrust them to reliable people, who will be able to teach others also.'[14]

Teach the scriptures

The third aspect of the teaching of the pastoral epistles was that Paul's young co-workers had to trust and to teach the scriptures.

The problem with false teachers stemmed from the fact that they did not understand the scriptures, despite the fact that they spoke about the Law with such confidence. The answer lay in a proper understanding of the gospel which flows from a knowledge of the scriptures. Paul stressed that sound teaching 'is found in the gospel that was entrusted to me to announce, the good news from the glorious and blessed God.'[15]

Here Paul gave one of the most beautiful insights we have into the nature of scripture:

Continue in the truths that you were taught and firmly believe. You know who your teachers were, and you remember that ever since you were a child you have known the holy scriptures, which are able to give you the wisdom that leads to salvation through faith in Christ Jesus. All scripture is inspired by God and is useful for teaching the truth, rebuking error, correcting faults and giving instruction for right living, so that the person who serves God may be fully qualified and equipped to do every kind of good deed.[16]

Timothy here is given the task to preach sound doctrine from the scriptures and to make sure other people followed it, being faithful even as Paul was to death. Paul constantly distinguishes between the faithful Timothy who continues in the scriptures, and others who are evil and who add their own concepts to the scriptural basis of truth. Every generation faces the temptation to add to the scriptures new understanding and interpretation that is simply humanist or man-centred reasoning. Paul's thinking was that Timothy could safeguard himself by testing his own new thoughts against those of Paul who had taught him the faith.

This use of the apostle's life and thought as the test for orthodoxy was not egoism. This was true of each of the apostles: those who had been closest to Jesus were in themselves yardsticks against whom the young believers should check their words and actions. There is a consistency about Christian teaching. What is written is seen in the life of the Master and those who knew him and were appointed by him to be apostles. Christian teaching can be read both in words and character. The test we have is to align our words with those of the scriptures, and our characters with those of the Master and his apostles.

Paul asserts that all scripture is 'inspired', or 'breathed' by God. The Holy Spirit filled the mind of the writers, including Paul's, so what they wrote was guided by God. Their individual personality and differing perspective gave variety to their work, but the Spirit's presence within them gave their writing its quality, consistency and authority. That is what makes it useful and profitable, both for our believing and our conduct.

Communicating with young people

Paul knew how to communicate to his young co-workers. In fact, these pastoral epistles appeal to young people in general. Paul took the young person's interest in athletics and made several comments about the sport. There were great stadiums for athletics, not only in the areas in which the young men had travelled, but also where they were ministering. Paul wrote:

Keep yourself in training for a godly life. Physical exercise has some value, but spiritual exercise is valuable in every way, because it promises life both for the present and for the future. Run your best in the race of faith, and win eternal life for yourself; for it was to this life that God called you when you firmly professed your faith before many witnesses. An athlete who runs in a race cannot win a prize unless he obeys the rules.

As for me, the hour has come for me to be sacrificed; the time is here for me to leave this life. I have done my best in the race, I have run the full distance, and I have kept the faith. And now there is waiting for me the prize of victory awarded to a righteous life, the prize which the Lord, the righteous judge, will give me on that Day — and not only to me, but to all those who wait with love for him to appear.[17]

Paul also used another analogy that young people understood. It had to do with a farmer who planted seed in preparation for the harvest. He wanted Timothy and Titus to work hard and be workmen who could look back

with a sense of satisfaction on hard work knowing it brought a good reward:

The farmer who has done the hard work should have the first share of the harvest. . . Do your best to win full approval in God's sight, as a worker who is not ashamed of his work, one who correctly teaches the message of God's truth . . . Keep away from foolish and ignorant arguments; you know that they end up in quarrels. The Lord's servant must not quarrel. He must be kind towards all, a good and patient teacher who is gentle as he corrects his opponents, for it may be that God will give them the opportunity to repent and come to know the truth.[18]

In Australia, more than most countries, there was little respect for a minister of religion in the early days, but great respect for the man who was a 'fair dinkum parson'. The famous Australian writer, Henry Lawson, once wrote about such a man. He said the Australian farmer seldom raised his hat to anybody and when the bush parson came round the men would judge him by how he cared for his horse. Henry Lawson told of Peter McLaughlan, who used to visit in the outback. 'The bushman will seldom lift his hat to any man, but out there in the west, even the worst of characters used to listen bare-headed when Peter McLaughlan preached.'

That was the highest tribute the men could pay — they recognised a workman of God who had no need to be ashamed. It seems that Timothy and Titus had the same respect. It was men like that to whom we owe the success of the young church.

For personal reading

Theme: Partners in the gospel

MONDAY
: Teach right doctrine
1 Timothy 1:3-7; 4:1-5

TUESDAY
: Encourage others
1 Timothy 1:12-14; 4:11 — 5:22

WEDNESDAY
: Teach others to teach
2 Timothy 2:2-7

THURSDAY
: Work hard
2 Timothy 2:15; 3:1-9

FRIDAY
: Trust the scriptures
2 Timothy 3:10-17

SATURDAY
: Preach the message
2 Timothy 4:1-5

SUNDAY
: The Christian life
Titus 2:1-10

For group study

Topic: Training for the teaching ministry

1 How important was Timothy's upbringing as preparation for his later ministry?

2 What teaching of Paul would Timothy think about when he saw a stadium?

3 How relevant is Paul's teaching to Timothy in 1 Timothy 4:11 — 5:22 today?

4 What does Paul teach about teaching others?

5 Paul praised Titus for his capacity as a minister. What do you think young ministers could learn from the life of Titus?

7

The Hebrews

From the time of the Emperor Claudius onward the Jews suffered serious persecution at the hands of the Romans. The Roman army forced the Jews out of their land, out of Rome and out of other major cities. Their distinctiveness made the Jews easy targets for repression, suspicion and persecution. Jewish Christians, who were predominant in the early church, suffered similar persecution.

The letter to the Hebrews was written to a group of Jewish Christians who lived in Rome in spite of the expulsion order, and was circulated among other Jewish Christians who had been excluded from their homeland. Greetings were sent from the Italian Jews who had to flee from Rome.

The persecutions

The Christians in Jerusalem suffered constant persecution throughout the first forty years of the church's existence. Immediately after the crucifixion of Jesus, Peter, James and John and the other disciples faced imprisonment and persecution.

Paul, then known as Saul, was harassing the church, dragging believers off to gaol and Stephen was stoned to death. The persecution continued throughout Jerusalem and Judea, causing many Christians to flee to outlying, safer areas. Saul's decision to follow them to Damascus was due to the fact that so many of them had escaped the persecution.

Even in Rome they found no security. Some of the Jewish Christians went to Rome following the day of Pentecost, but even there they found continued harassment. The movement of Priscilla and Aquila to Corinth, where they met with Paul and became foundation members of to the new church, and to Ephesus where they also met with Paul and the established believers, may have been due to persecution. Some of the early Christians had to keep moving because of fresh outbreaks of local hostility.

Five years after the expulsion under Claudius, the harassed Jews started to drift back into the centre of the empire once more and slowly their numbers built up until the disastrous fire of Rome on 19 July AD 64. Nero blamed the Christians and commenced a bloody persecution in which both Peter and Paul were martyred. Once more Christian Jews died and were scattered abroad. This, however, was a local persecution and safety was found in other cities of the empire.

In Palestine, the persecution took a different turn. Caesarea was a coastal recreation area for Roman soldiers. It was here the Roman centurion Cornelius, converted by Peter, was stationed. Here, Paul was imprisoned and tried before Festus and Herod Agrippa. It became a centre where believers died for the amusement of off-duty soldiers who liked to gamble on the results of the fighting of gladiators.

One of the finest Roman theatres in the Middle East stands at Caesarea. It seats 25,000 today and was the scene for concerts and plays. Nearby, as yet unexcavated, is a stadium of immense size. There were international games organised here every five years and it was the site of the 192nd Olympiad.

The amphitheatre provided entertainment and diversion for the many Roman soldiers stationed there. It was a huge construction, larger than the Colosseum in Rome, the inside

track measuring over three hundred feet in length. Gladiatorial contests were held here, the first being organised by Herod in 10 BC. The Roman general, later emperor, Titus, ordered hundreds of Jewish prisoners of war to be killed here in gladiatorial contests and among them were large numbers of Christians. From AD 66 Vespasian, tough, shrewd commander of Roman legions who suppressed the Jewish rebellion and his successor, Titus, sought to destroy the Jews. Titus utterly destroyed Jerusalem in AD 70, dismantling every building and pushing every block and building stone and brick over the edge of the walls down into the Valley Kedron. Not one stone of Jerusalem was left standing, thereby unwittingly fulfilling the prophecy Jesus made about the city of Jerusalem.

As the Jews scattered from Jerusalem to other parts of the Roman Empire, Vespasian was recalled to Rome where he became Emperor. Now, as Emperor, his hatred for the Hebrews had an international stage for execution, and across the Empire the Jews, including the Christian Jews, were to suffer for their birthright.

One of the emperor Vespasian's greatest building accomplishments was the building of the Colosseum. He brought thousands of Jewish and Christian prisoners-of-war to Rome as slaves to build this huge memorial to his family and dynasty. By AD 79 he had dedicated the first two storeys of this huge amphitheatre.

The floor of the arena was covered with timber which covered the cells of both the wild beasts and the victims of the gladiators. These were to be torn to death in this arena for the amusement of the crowd and officials who sat in the Emperor's box. Forty-five thousand spectators could fill this arena where they enjoyed the spectacle of Christians and Jews being butchered.

These Jewish Christian slaves had to work to build the monument to man's inhumanity to man. They were then murdered for sport before the roaring crowds. Ironically, later popes had the stones dressed and hauled and rebuilt into the Cathedral of St Peter. As the blood of martyrs became the seed of the church, so the sweat of the martyrs became the cement of the cathedral.

The underground church

To escape the authorities and the threats of persecution, Roman Christians hid in underground tunnels and caves cut in the soft volcanic tufa used originally as burial chambers. There are more than forty such catacombs around Rome covering about eight hundred kilometres of tunnels and ledges upon which the bodies of the faithful were laid to rest. The ledges were closed by a marble, stone or brick slab on which was written the name and expression of faith of the person buried within.

The earliest burials in the discovered catacombs were not until about AD 150 — which prohibits the popular conception of Peter and Paul both meeting

with persecuted Christians in the catacombs, unless there were smaller, as yet unidentified, catacombs within the city limits.

The catacombs were important sources of early examples of Christian art, and words and prayers of the faithful are written on the walls. The traditional symbols of anchors, ships, fish, crosses, chi rhos, and pictures of the Good Shepherd carrying a lamb were all commonly used. Unfortunately, most of the historical wealth of the catacombs has been carried off into the Vatican museum where it can be seen, but not in its natural environment.

During this century, in three widely separated areas of the ancient world — Cirencester in England, Dura-Europos on the Euphrates River, and Pompeii in Italy — a secret Christian sign has been found which is dated before the eruption of Mt Vesuvius in AD 79. It is known as the ROTAS-SATOR word square. The words can be be spelt in each direction:

```
R  O  T  A  S
O  P  E  R  A
T  E  N  E  T
A  R  E  P  O
S  A  T  O  R
```

This strange sentence which means 'The wheels with care hold Arepo the Sower,' or 'Arepo the sower holds the wheels with care' is an allusion to Ezekial 10:2 where the angels hold the coals of fire from the wheels of God's judgment chariot. It could be a statement of faith about God's coming judgment upon the Roman persecutors.

At the centre of all sides of the word square is the letter T, the ancient symbol of the cross. This letter also appears centrally placed twice in two occurrences of *PATERNOSTER*, 'Our Father', the first two words of The Lord's Prayer, together with A and O, the letters used by Christ to describe himself as alpha and omega, the beginning and the end:

```
                  A

                  P

                  A

                  T

                  E

                  R
A  P A T E R  N  O S T E R  O

                  O

                  S

                  T

                  E

                  R

                  O
```

During the persecutions, this word square may have been used to teach the faith, as a symbol of defiance, or as a secret sign of recognition between the believers.

The early church was born in blood and persecution and one of their choicest encouragements was the letter that circulated among the Hebrew Christians called *The Epistle to the Hebrews*. Its message was of special interest to the Jewish Christians and told how Jesus had fulfilled the Messianic promises, how the Old Testament Law was fulfilled in him, and how he wanted them to stand fast in their faith.

The Letter to the Hebrews was probably written before AD 70 as there is no mention of the destruction of the temple in Jerusalem, which would have strongly supported its argument in favour of the Old Testament sacrificial system being outmoded. When speaking of the Temple the author consistently uses the present tense indicating the Temple is still in Jerusalem. It speaks about the former days of persecution and so was probably written in the late sixties. As it is quoted in 1 Clement 36:1-5, it must have been in circulation for some good time before AD 95.

The author

The Epistle to the Hebrews has been an enigma. It has been attributed to Paul, although from earliest times this has been disputed. The literary style is not the rugged style of Paul's letters, for this letter stands with the writings of Luke for its polished presentation.

The early fathers recognised that it was probably written by a person well acquainted with Paul and so Barnabas and Luke were suggested. Barnabas is a likely suggestion, as he was well versed in the scriptures, was a priest of the tribe of Levi, was close to Paul and possessed the authority of the early church. He was mentioned early as the author by Tertullian.

Martin Luther suggested the author was possibly Apollos who was familiar with Paul's thought, was a man of great eloquence who knew the Old Testament well, particularly the Alexandrian Septuagint version of the Old Testament (for all quotes are from it), and who had a feeling for Greek logic which marks the way the letter is carefully composed and argued. Origen stated bluntly, according to Eusebius, that only God knew who wrote it.

Because of doubts about the author, some of the early church fathers argued that it should not be included in the New Testament, but the uniqueness of its argument and content, its helpfulness to many of the faithful under stress and its exaltation of Christ gave sufficient grounds for its inclusion.

It is not even an epistle, technically. It has few of the characteristics of a letter: it lacks an address, a recipient, a signature, the usual introduction and the form of a letter. It is more like a polished sermon on a specific theme.

Even the title was added later, as the recipients were unknown.

But it was obviously addressed to Hebrew Christians who were under persecution, and who from their knowledge of the Old Testament were being confirmed in their faith under severe trial.

The purpose and message

Its purpose is mentioned in these closing words: 'Listen patiently to this message of encouragement'.[1]

As those early Jewish Christians fled under persecution to the remote parts of the empire, they passed round copies of this letter which encouraged them and their fellow believers throughout the empire.

The theological argument centres on the supremacy of Christ who is seen as God's final word to us. Christ is demonstrated as superior to their old Jewish ways, beliefs and practices. In fact, the word 'superior' is used thirteen times.

The writer argues that Jesus is superior to everything within the Jewish past. He is superior to the prophets of the Old Testament because he is God's last and greatest word to mankind; he is superior to the angels for they are his servants; and he is superior to Moses for Moses was a servant of God whereas Jesus was the Son.[2]

In the same manner he is superior to Joshua, for while the great Joshua brought people into a promised land, Jesus brings people into eternal rest.[3] Jesus was superior to Aaron, for though Aaron developed the priesthood, Jesus Christ was the great high priest who offered himself as a sacrifice once and for all to take away the sins of the world.[4]

Christ is superior even to Melchizedek, who was superior to

Abraham, the father of the race and of faith. Christ was superior in his birth, was indestructible in death (because of the resurrection) and was in himself prophet, priest and king. As well, Christ introduced a new covenant superior to the old covenant, a new sanctuary and a new sacrifice which was himself.[5]
His role as our great high priest is demonstrated in the following.

We have, then, my brothers, complete freedom to go into the Most Holy Place by means of the death of Jesus. He opened for us a new way, a living way, through the curtain — that is, through his own body. We have a great high priest in charge of the house of God. So let us come near to God with a sincere heart and a sure faith, with hearts that have been purified from a guilty conscience and with bodies washed with clean water. Let us hold on firmly to the hope we profess, because we can trust God to keep his promise. Let us be concerned for one another, to help one another to show love and to do good. Let us not give up the habit of meeting together, as some are doing. Instead let us encourage one another all the more, since you see that the Day of the Lord is coming nearer.[6]

Jesus is proclaimed as God's last and ultimate word. He is superior to anything in heaven or on earth; superior to any previous prophet or priest; superior to any other covenant, sacrifice or hope. He is Lord. As a consequence we who believe in him must live in faith with dedication and commitment in our daily conduct.[7]
The short exhortations to the

hearers, with which each theological section concludes, are of great interest. They were answering a need, and an examination of the answers indicates the need. The exhortations are to 'keep up our courage and our confidence in what we hope for', to be 'partners with Christ if we hold firmly to the end the confidence we had at the beginning', not to 'lose your courage, then, for it brings with it a great reward', nor be 'people who turn back and are lost. Instead, we have faith and are saved.'[8] And the epistle ends with the great exhortation to 'run with determination the race that lies before us. Let us keep our eyes fixed on Jesus, on whom our faith depends from beginning to end'.[9]

Apparently, then, some believers had become discouraged, were neglecting their faith, were lacking confidence, were turning back, dropping out and giving up. The letter was to provide them with scriptural evidence of how Jesus was indeed the Christ and superior to the old Law, and personal encouragement to keep to their faith in spite of the difficulties and persecutions they faced.

The final message of Hebrews is to remind them of the faithfulness of other believers in days gone by, and to encourage them to stand fast under their own persecution:

Remember how it was with you in the past. In those days, after God's light had shone on you, you suffered many things, yet were not defeated by the struggle. You were at times publicly insulted and ill-treated, and at other times you were ready to join

those who were being treated in this way You shared the sufferings of prisoners, and when all your belongings were seized, you endured your loss gladly, because you knew that you still possessed something much better, which would last for ever. Do not lose your courage, then, because it brings with it a great reward.[10]

In order to point out that their persecution enables them to stand in line with the great fathers of the faith who also suffered for what they believed, the book provides a great roll-call of faithful people from Abel, Enoch, Noah, Abraham, Isaac, Jacob, Joseph, Moses, right down to themselves.

The letter concludes with one of the most beautiful words of encouragement in the whole Bible:

Through faith they fought whole countries and won. They did what was right and received what God had promised. They shut the mouths of lions, put out fierce fires, escaped being killed by the sword. They were weak, but became strong; they were mighty in battle and defeated the armies of foreigners. Through faith women received their dead relatives raised back to life.

Others, refusing to accept freedom, died under torture in order to be raised to a better life. Some were mocked and whipped, and others were put in chains and taken off to prison. They were stoned, they were sawn in two, they were killed by the sword. They went around clothed in skins of sheep or goats — poor, persecuted, and ill-treated. The world was not good enough for them! They wandered like refugees in the deserts and hills, living in caves and holes in the ground.

What a record all of these have won by their faith! . . . As for us, we have this large crowd of witnesses round us. So then, let us rid ourselves of everything that gets in the way, and of the sin which holds on to us so tightly, and let us run with determination the race that lies before us. Let us keep our eyes fixed on Jesus, on whom our faith depends from beginning to end. He did not give up because of the cross! On the contrary, because of the joy that was waiting for him, he thought nothing of the disgrace and dying on the cross, and he is now seated at the right-hand side of God's throne.

What a letter of encouragement! Out of the tragedy of persecution they saw God's plan for the future being beautifully woven.

For personal reading

Theme: Christ our role-model

MONDAY	The leaders *Acts 8:1; 9:1-2; 11:19; 12:1-18*
TUESDAY	Reason for writing *Hebrews 1:1-4*
WEDNESDAY	The inferiority of the Law *Hebrews 10:1-10*
THURSDAY	Christ the new way *Hebrews 10:19-25*
FRIDAY	The future reward *Hebrews 10:32-39*
SATURDAY	Faithful examples *Hebrews 11:4 — 12:2*
SUNDAY	Enduring persecution *Hebrews 12:12-29*

For group study

Topic: The price of faithfulness

1   How does the writer of the letter to the Hebrews encourage Christians under persecution?

2   'The Church expands best under persecution.' Discuss this.

3   If the Roman Empire had embraced Christianity in the first century, do you think that would have meant a more effective spreading of the gospel?

4   How can the message of Hebrews be applied to churches not under persecution? Is it possible for an effective church not to come under persecution?

5   What can we learn from the people mentioned in Hebrews 11?

8

John

John was with his friend Andrew when they first heard about Jesus of Nazareth. They were both fishermen and they had been listening to John the Baptist down by the river Jordan where it enters the Dead Sea. John the Baptist had pointed them toward Jesus and Jesus had invited them to come and follow him. Simon Peter was also called later that day, so these three fishermen, John, Andrew and Simon Peter, were the first disciples.

Later, back up along the shores of the Sea of Galilee, Jesus again came to them. This time John was working with his brother James and with Zebedee, his father, in

their large fishing boats. Zebedee was fairly wealthy and employed a number of fishermen as well as servants. Jesus called them to leave their nets, follow him and learn to 'catch men'. And immediately they left their father Zebedee in the boat with the hired men and went with Jesus.[1] John was not to know that that decision to leave his work as a fisherman was going to change the rest of his life and give him seventy years of incredible hardship and happiness.

John was high-spirited, zealous and impetuous. With his brother, they were nicknamed 'the sons of thunder' for their capacity to shout and lose their tempers. The two sets of brothers — Andrew and Simon Peter, and James and John — became the nucleus within the band of disciples.

Frequently scripture mentions that Peter, James and John went ahead with Jesus and they formed a close personal band. They were together at the transfiguration of Jesus when God revealed that Jesus was his Son. The three of them went with Jesus into the inner room of Jairus' house when Jesus raised his little daughter from the dead.

It was the same three that were with Jesus in the last moments of

The Sea of Galilee

prayer in the Garden of Gethsemane. Jesus needed close friends and John was his closest. John and Peter prepared the upper room for the Passover meal the night that Jesus was betrayed and, at the table, John sat next to Jesus.

The next day, when Jesus was crucified, only one disciple remained at the cross and that was John. It was into John's care that Jesus entrusted his widowed mother Mary, and John took her into his own house.[2] If John's mother, Salome, was the same Salome who was with Mary at the cross, then she was the sister of Mary. It was therefore natural that Jesus should commit the care of his mother into the hands of John, and for John to care for his aunt.[3] Tradition indicates that John cared for Mary throughout the rest of her life and she travelled with him to Ephesus, where he ministered. There is strong local tradition that Mary died there, and the supposed burial site has been sacred for centuries.

On the morning of the resurrection, Peter and John ran to the tomb on hearing that the great stone had been rolled away and that Jesus was not in the tomb. John got there first, but he did not go into the tomb. The older Peter rushed straight in and saw the empty shelf upon which the dead body of Jesus had lain. It was John who believed first in the resurrection and was first to recognise the risen Jesus on the seashore.

When the church was established on the day of Pentecost, John and Peter proclaimed that Jesus had risen from the dead and was able to forgive the sins of those that believed in him. Immediately they were imprisoned and this was the first of a lifetime of difficulties, the price of that witness.

Shortly after this, John's brother, James, was murdered by Herod Agrippa the First, so becoming the first disciple to be martyred. John stayed in Jerusalem and continued to witness to his faith for a number of years, being known as one of the pillars of the church.

After the mention of his name in Acts 8, John is not again mentioned in Acts, and is only once mentioned by Paul, soon after Paul's conversion. Most of our knowledge of his life, writings and death comes from tradition recorded by early historians. They do not give us a great deal of factual information, although Theophylact indicates he was punished under the persecution of the Emperor Nero, and the most reliable of the historians — Irenaeus, Eusebius and Jerome — all attest to the fact that he was exiled on the island of Patmos during the persecution of the Emperor Domitian. Five consecutive emperors persecuted the church during the lifetime of John.

Pastor in Ephesus

Some years later, John travelled from Jerusalem to be the pastor of what became a powerful church in the city of Ephesus. Ephesus was one of the great Roman cities on the western shore of Turkey by the Aegean Sea.

Paul had established the church in Ephesus and had ministered there personally for three years, the longest of any of his ministries, from AD 52 to 55. From Ephesus, Paul sent out younger ministers to evangelise

Ephesus

the surrounding valleys and the villages and towns along the nearby rivers. So systematic and sweeping was this outreach from Ephesus that 'all the people who lived in the province of Asia, both Jews and Gentiles, heard the word of the Lord.'[4] Peter also had contact with the churches in the area, yet the records of the church historians all centre round the pre-eminence of John's influence.

Since the earliest of times, there has been some confusion over the authorship of the Gospel, the epistles and Revelation. Tradition is strong that all the works emanated from Ephesus, although scholars assign the three works to various authors with little agreement except that different authors from the same circle or school under the influence of John the apostle may be involved.

Ephesus was the city of the Temple of Artemis, the largest building in the world. It had a beautiful natural harbour which has long since silted up. It was the major city and gateway into Asia and housed the largest bank in the empire. It had also been the centre of opposition to Paul and of riots against Paul and his co-workers.

The evidence of history
In Ephesus John ministered among the people for decades, until advanced old age. All of the early church historians like Irenaeus, Eusebius, Papias and Dionysius, who wrote not long after John's death, referred to his ministry in this great city. There is little doubt concerning the accuracy of this fact.

Dionysius, the bishop of Alexandria, at the end of the second century argued that the John who names himself as the author of Revelation was a disciple of John the apostle who wrote the Gospel, and quoted as evidence that both of their tombs were in Ephesus.

Evidence of an early
Christian community in Ephesus

Papias came from Pontus and was bishop of Hierapolis, in the Lycus Valley, not far from Ephesus, during the first half of the second century. He claimed to have been a hearer of John and a contemporary of Polycarp. His five volumes have been lost, but passages have ben quoted by Eusebius and Irenaeus. Papias spoke of 'the elders of the faith', meaning those second generation Christians who were hearers of the words of the disciples, but includes among them John the Elder. He may be referring to the apostle who by advanced age was known as 'the elder' or to a separate John in Ephesus who had been a disciple of the apostle John.

Bishop Eusebius believed that there were two named John in Ephesus, one John the apostle and the other John the Elder. Clement of Alexandria indicated that the apostle John moved from Patmos to Ephesus after the Emperor Domitian's death. Irenaeus, who came from the area near Ephesus, claims to have heard Polycarp, who died a martyr in AD 156, saying he had been appointed as Bishop of Smyrna by the apostles, but particularly by John. Polycrates, who was bishop of Ephesus at the end of the second century, stated that the apostle John died in Ephesus where he was buried.

Certainly, by the time of Emperor Constantine in the fourth century, a large church was built upon the site of his burial. By the Council of Ephesus in AD 431, Augustine was reporting the rumour that the ground over John's grave moved up and down in time to the saint's breathing.

Ephesus

I have visited the huge remains of the basilica in Ephesus, built by Emperor Justinian (AD 527-565) to honour St John the Divine. It was built over an early church perhaps built by Constantine the Great, and beneath the foundations of this earlier church can still be seen the burial vault which lay beneath the original altar.

This custom of burying a saint beneath the altar was also observed in both of the original churches built over the burial places of Paul and Peter. When new basilicas were built, the remains of the saints were shifted to a new resting place beneath the main altar. This happened with St Peter's, Rome, and recently remains of Peter's tomb were uncovered during some reconstruction work beneath the main altar.

The evidence for the authorship of the Gospel, the epistles and Revelation is still the subject of contemporary debate. Professors C.H. Dodd, W.F. Howard, J. Massyngberde Ford, Oscar Cullmann, and C.K. Barratt have all written scholarly and differing interpretations in the last few decades.

Some see the apostle John as the author of Revelation with the epistles and the Gospel being written by members of his circle of disciples, one or more of whom may have also been called John the Elder. This John the Elder succeeded John the apostle and led the circle of Christian leaders influenced by the apostle in Ephesus.

Because the evidence and the scholarship is so divided on this issue of authorship, which lies outside the purpose of this book,

we will use the term 'John' to mean the author of all five books bearing his name, and identifying him with the apostle John. I prefer the view that they were written by a Johannine circle who wrote in the spirit of the apostle.

The Gospel of John

It was in Ephesus that 'the disciple whom Jesus loved', as John referred to himself, wrote the great Gospel that bore his name. It was written before the destruction of Jerusalem, which occurred in AD 70. The Gospel was the result of John's thirty or more years of mature thinking about those three years he spent travelling with Jesus listening to his teaching. He wrote with intimacy and personal knowledge of the events surrounding the life of Jesus.

His own Jewish background flows out of his writings as he speaks about key ideas from the Old Testament — about word, life, light, shepherd, spirit, bread, vine and love. There are many

semitic literary touches, such as the use of parallelisms, where a teaching is repeated paralleling the first presentation. He gives us a great deal of eyewitness detail and personal information on minor characters involved in the life of Jesus. He mentions every disciple by name except himself. He presents eyewitness details of the Last Supper.

In the last two decades, it has been revealed that John shares with the writers of the Dead Sea Scrolls some parallel texts, which is understandable since he and they had access to the Old Testament. Like the Essenes, John knew the land well and the religious-cultural milieu in which they lived.

The Dead Sea Scrolls have many teachings that are not compatible with New Testament teachings. The disciples believed that Jesus was the Messiah who had come as a suffering servant to redeem Israel, whereas the Essenes were looking to the fulfilment of Mosaic Law by an all-conquering messiah. Salvation for the Essenes was only for a few who were the elect because they were children of the light, whereas the disciples preached salvation by faith in Jesus as Christ.

The Scrolls have many similar features to that of the Gospel of John in that they emphasise sin, repentance and baptism by water and by spirit. This is, of course, reflected in the teaching of John the Baptist who probably came from this community, and who was baptising in the Jordan only a few kilometres to the northeast. John's Gospel gives the fullest account of the teaching of The Baptist.

Cave at Qumran

The Essenes also saw the world as a scene of the conflict between good and evil, light and darkness, truth and falsehood, all themes developed in John's Gospel. Their concepts of dualism between the sons of light and the sons of darkness go far beyond the emphasis found in the Gospel or the epistles, but they are still there and in conflict with each other, as are the forces of truth and falsehood. John's use of the themes of 'the light of life' and 'the sons of light' are both phrases found among the Essene writings.

What can be made of this is that in the time when Jesus came preaching, there was a widespread community interest in a vital religious truth and in re-interpreting the Old Testament. The vital interpretation of religious truth in the Jewish community indicates that earlier attempts of scholars to align New Testament teaching with Greek traditions are utterly unnecessary.

John's prologue to his Gospel, one of the finest pieces of

Laodicea

religious writing known, parallels the Essene beliefs that light, truth and wisdom were there in the beginning of creation with God. John went further to indicate that these concepts were the eternal Christ himself.

The oldest manuscripts in existence that quote the Gospel, even if in fragment, attest to John's authorship: The Rylands Papyrus 457 and the Egerton Papyrus (both written before AD 150). Early Gnostic writers knew John as the author, as did all of the early church historians.

John stated quite clearly his purpose in writing: 'these have been written in order that you may believe that Jesus is the Messiah, the Son of God, and that through your faith in him, you may have life.'[5] The whole point of John's writing was that people would understand that Jesus was the Word of God made flesh, the Messiah, the Son of God, and that those who heard this news might obey and love him as did John and the other disciples.

The Gospel he wrote was carefully structured. He mentions seven miracles which were signs that Jesus was sent by God to be the Messiah, and seven 'I am' passages. Of all Gospels, this is the one with the greatest spiritual understanding and teaching.

The Epistles of John

John wrote three letters from Ephesus. He writes as 'the Elder', one of the pieces of internal evidence that suggests the author is different from that of the Gospel. The letters may have been written by another John in Ephesus who was close to John the apostle but who used the terminology 'the Elder' to differentiate himself.

He writes to protect the younger believers who are his 'beloved little children'. The time is urgent because there are some false teachers who are active in the fellowship and some false prophets and deceivers who are attempting to lead the believers away from the path of truth. He writes forcefully, pointing out the errors of those teachers who deny that Jesus is the Son of God who came in flesh to save humankind. He speaks against false prophets, deceivers, 'anti-Christs' and incorrect teaching and denies Jesus' pre-existence, real incarnation and the provision of his salvation.

The last two of the three letters were shorter notes, just long enough to fill a standard piece of papyrus. One was written to a church and the other to a church leader concerning matters of personal relationships that troubled the members of a local church.

The Revelation of John

The persecutions that swept across the Roman world following Nero, under the leadership of Roman emperors like Vespasian and Domitian, caused much suffering and anguish for the early Christians and for John himself. Nero's persecution had been confined to Rome itself, but the succeeding emperors launched a persecution that covered the empire. The persecutions of Nero had been sporadic, but those that followed were systematic. Even to claim the name of Christ was enough to bring execution during the period of bitter persecutions.

John suffered greatly, being dropped into a vat of boiling oil but, according to the early historian Tertullian, he survived without serious injury. John was then sent into exile on the island of Patmos, a windswept rocky island off the coast of Turkey. The emperor Domitian banished his niece Flavia Domitilla to a small island, Pontia, and executed her husband because they had been converted. Her nobleman husband from the royal household may be the 'most excellent Theophilus' to whom Luke wrote his Gospel and Acts.

Such punishment may have been confiscation of all property and civil rights and banishment from family and friends for life, known in later centuries as 'transportation for the term of his natural life'. If this was so, then John would have been free to move round the island, to earn a living, and to study, write and pray. Some significant political prisoners were treated in this fashion.

This small, volcanic island in the south-east Aegean is only forty kilometres in circumference. It is fairly barren. On the south side of the island is the traditional cave where John is believed to have written his revelation. Above it today lies the monastery of St John the Divine. Looking out from the cave, one can see the sea stretching to the horizon, and beyond it to the east lies Turkey, sixty kilometres away. The sea plays a significant part in John's writings, and in Revelation the sea is mentioned twenty-five times.

On the island of Patmos John was separated from the Christians in Turkey who were also suffering for their faith. It was while he was there he had a vision of Jesus risen from the dead who was still lord of history and who would triumph over the Romans and all the worst that they could do.

His main concern, therefore, was to convey a message of encouragement to others who were suffering persecution and to remind them to be faithful and to live with hope. But apart from calling the believers to be faithful under persecution, John also wanted to correct the rise of doctrinal error and immoral behaviour. The churches were under internal threat as well as external persecution.

John's letter had a special message for the Christians in the seven churches that were established in the main cities within a radius of 150 miles of Ephesus. He said:

I am John, your brother, and as a follower of Jesus I am your partner in patiently enduring the suffering that comes to those who belong to his kingdom. I was put on the island of Patmos because I had proclaimed God's word and the truth that Jesus revealed. On the Lord's Day the Spirit took control of me, and I heard a loud voice that sounded like a trumpet, speaking behind me. It said, 'write down what you see, and send the book to the churches in the seven cities of Ephesus, Smyrna, Pergamum, Thyatira, Sardis, Philadelphia, and Laodicea.[6]

His book was visionary, like a dream of what would be happening in the future, and underlining it all was the tremendous insight into how God is in control.

After some years of exile, John was released from the island of Patmos and allowed to return to Ephesus. This probably happened at the end of the reign of Domitian when Nerva became for a brief period emperor and acted with more clemency towards people who had been imprisoned during his predecessor's reign.

The old man, now in his nineties, returned to the people whom he had encouraged during the dark days of persecution. He was to live for several more years, dying peacefully during the time of Trajan, which meant some time after AD 98.

One of the early church historians, Irenaeus, said that in advanced old age and weakness, he was frequently carried to meetings where he would always greet the believers with the statement, 'little children, love one another'. The grand old apostle of love had come a long way from the time when, as a young man, he and his brother were named 'sons of thunder'.

Each of the Gospel writers was given a symbol representing their special contribution to the life of the church. The symbol of John has always been an eagle. Many large brass eagle Bible stands are in churches around the world. John was given the eagle because it was said of all creatures the eagle is the only one to be able to look directly into the face of the sun without blinking. So John the apostle, in the most spiritual writing of all the Gospels, looked directly into the face of the Son of God and wrote for us eternal truth.

For personal reading

Theme: An apostle remembers

MONDAY
John's call
John 1:35-37, Mark 3:13-19

TUESDAY
After the resurrection
John 20:1-10; 21:20-23

WEDNESDAY
John's test of righteousness
1 John 1:5 — 2:6

THURSDAY
Victory through faith
1 John 5:1-4

FRIDAY
John in exile
Revelation 1:1-10

SATURDAY
Strength during persecution
1 Peter 4:12-19

SUNDAY
John's test of love
1 John 2:7-17

For group study

Topic: The apostle of love

1   From the Gospel accounts, what picture emerges of the sort of person that John was?

2   What arguments does John use in the Gospel to show that Jesus was who he claimed he was?

3   What was the key emphasis in John's ministry?

4   According to 1 John 2:7-17, what is the test of true faith?

5   How would you react to the suffering endured by John and the other Christians during the reign of Nero and the following emperors?

9

The Seven Churches: Ephesus and Smyrna

In the last third of the first century AD the Roman Empire was trying to consolidate its political unity by forcing everybody to worship Caesar. The early Christians refused to say 'Caesar is Lord' because they believed 'Jesus Christ is Lord'. Consequently, throughout the ancient world they were persecuted, hounded and murdered. Their unwillingness to burn incense and say 'Caesar is Lord' meant that they were condemned for the rest of their lives.

Bust of Caesar

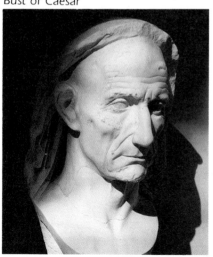

On the island of Patmos, John saw beyond the might of Rome to the certainty of the victory of Jesus Christ. He wrote down what he saw in what became known as *The Revelation of John the Divine* and he sent letters to the seven churches in Turkey which were situated just over the horizon.

Unique writings

A hundred years before John was born, a new kind of writing was developed in Israel called *apocalyptic literature*. The style of writing was different to anything that had ever been seen before. It was highly picturesque, and concerned not this present evil age which was beyond saving and unable to be reformed, but the age to come.

Apocalyptic writing indicated that God was sovereign and was in command over all history, that behind the activities of generals, merchants and politicians, God was still in control. Through a series of symbols and pictures expressing the inexpressible, God patiently worked out the future for those he loved. Those who read apocalyptic literature were generally people suffering under some tyrant or bloodthirsty emperor. The result of reading such literature, and understanding the special code in the form of images, was that the readers received great encouragement and hope.

Turkey's significance

The churches to which Revelation was sent were on the western side of Turkey. Turkey's position geographically was of great significance: it was the major trade route between the East and the West, and the land bridge for great migrations of people between Europe and Asia.

The city at the strategic, narrow entrance to the Black Sea was Byzantium, later Constantinople and, later still, Istanbul. For twenty-seven centuries it has stood sentinel on the Bosphorus. It is the fabled, mystic city. As the people say of themselves, 'If one had but a single glance to give the world, one should gaze at Istanbul.' Certainly, dawn over Istanbul while it is shrouded in mist with spires, minarets and domes glistening in the early light, is one of the traveller's great experiences.

For centuries, Constantinople was, after Rome, the second most powerful city in the world. Across the country administered from the capital, large powerful cities developed at suitable ports, in fertile valleys, at the sites of thermal springs, along the trade routes and by the mountain fortresses that guarded the country. From among these cities, seven were chosen by John because of the churches situated in them.

John, while confined to Patmos, one Sunday experienced a state of spiritual intensity he described as

The port of Kavalla, Turkey

'in the Spirit', where the Lord took control of him and spoke to him. He said:

I turned round to see who was talking to me, and I saw seven gold lamp-stands, and among them there was what looked like a human being, wearing a robe that reached to his feet, and a gold band around his chest. His hair was white as wool, or as snow, and his eyes blazed like fire; his feet shone like brass that has been refined and polished, and his voice sounded like a roaring waterfall.

He held seven stars in his right hand, and a sharp two-edged sword came out of his mouth. His face was as bright as the midday sun. When I saw him I fell down at his feet like a dead man. He placed his right hand on me and said, 'Don't be afraid! I am the first and the last. I am the living one! I was dead, but now I am alive for ever and ever. I have authority over death and the world of the dead!' [1]

The Lord as high priest, king and prophet was standing among seven lamp-stands, symbolic of the seven churches in Turkey that were faithfully keeping the light burning in the darkness of persecution, and in his hand he held seven stars, which were bishops, ministers and pastors of the churches in Turkey.

There were seven churches mentioned by John, all within 150 miles of Ephesus where John had ministered for so long, each on the circular road. The other six were Smyrna, Pergamum, Thyatira, Sardis, Philadelphia and Laodicea. Other cities nearby also had churches including Colossae, Hierapolis, Troas, Magnesia, Tralles and Cyzicus.

The Church at Ephesus

The people of Ephesus could picture the scene of the Lord appearing to John in majesty, for in their city was a huge marble statue of the Emperor Domitian, the scourge of the Christians. This statue was possibly used in the prevailing Caesar-worship. The vision of the greatness of Jesus as Lord countered this daily vision of the persecuting Caesar.

The largest of the seven cities, Ephesus, was only sixty miles eastwards over the horizon from where John wrote. It was by the site of the present city of Seljuk, and some beautiful remains of the city John knew have been restored by archeologists. The city lay at the mouth of the River Cayster,

between the sea and the Koressos mountain range.

It was a great centre commercially, for the trade routes moving through its streets and its great port admitted ships from the seven seas, but especially from Athens and Rome. The trade routes across the Aegean terminated in Ephesus, and the great trade roads from the River Euphrates came down the Maeander and Cayster River valleys to Ephesus. Strabo called her 'the greatest emporium of Asia'.

Its significance as a port was always under threat because of the silting of the harbour due to the massive erosion from the mountains caused by a policy of deforestation in many parts of the ancient world. Trees were valued as charcoal for the metal industries, and forests were cleared without replanting. The omnipresent goat ate out the smaller shrubs and over-cropping allowed the winter rains from the high mountains to sweep the topsoil into the harbour.

Several times the city had to be moved down towards deeper water. The harbour silted and became a bed of high reeds. Today, you can walk from the marble streets of the harbour-side of ancient Ephesus twelve kilometres through three metre high reeds before you reach the present coastline. At the time John was writing, the harbour was already badly silted and her best days of trade were behind her.

That it was a great city of commerce can been seen from the size of both of the markets, or agoras, which are divided by a chessboard pattern of streets. From the top market, you can walk down the marble street of the Curetes, past the ruins of patricians' houses, temples and public buildings with courtyards and fountains. The street was lined with statues of famous citizens and heroes.

The bottom *agora* was 111 metres square, surrounded with colonnades and covered with marble with a central sundial. Here food, animals, cloth, spices, slaves and tents were sold alongside craftsmen who made copperware, jewellery and pottery.

Ephesus was a great educational centre as can be seen by the marvellous library of Celsus. Built soon after the time of John, it demonstrates the importance of knowledge. The three-storey building was built over the tomb of a hero. It housed over 12,000 scrolls of papyri. Today, its facade of columns, niches, statues and doors at the top of a flight of nine steps, twenty-one metres wide, make it one of the great archeological sights of the world. The statues represented wisdom, virility, goodwill and knowledge.

It was a centre of religious worship with the temple of Artemis — or Diana as the Romans called her — dominating the flat plain. It was the largest building in the world and one of the seven wonders of the world. It was a huge structure from every aspect. It stood upon a platform 73 metres wide and 127 metres long. It was surrounded by one hundred columns each more than seventeen metres high. The temple was three times the size of the Parthenon in Athens. It was magnificently decorated in statues, paintings and gold and jewels from all over the known world. Ironically, nothing remains except a sad collection of roundels from various columns. Following its destruction in AD 262, everything was looted, demolished and carried off by armies, conquerors and local peasants who built their houses and sheep pens with the finest of materials.

The main altar was about seven metres square and behind it was the huge statue of Artemis, possibly carved from a meteorite. A good Roman copy of the many-breasted goddess, the symbol of nourishing nature, today stands in the museum nearby. She has a temple and a basket upon her head, her arms are in long

Artemis or Diana

Roman reliefs found in Ephesus

embroidered sleeves, and her legs are covered in carvings of animals and bees. A large rectangular stone, once the base of a huge statue of Artemis, was recovered by archeologists and it today bears the carved sign of the cross with this inscription: 'Demeas removed the deceitful image of the demon Artemis and put in its place this sign which drives idols away, to the praise of God and the Cross, the victorious, imperishable symbol of Christ.'

The decline in the sales of souvenirs of this statue of the goddess, caused by Paul's preaching, resulted in a riot that ended up in the magnificent theatre, beautifully restored today and still able to seat 24,550 people. Holes round the stage held demountable iron bars for wild animal acts, and Paul's comment that he 'fought wild beasts in Ephesus' was probably literal.[2]

It was a political centre with the Roman government governing the whole region from these streets. Large houses, with beautiful mosaic floors, frescoed walls and painted ceilings tell of the luxury of these political leaders. Some houses average one hundred square metres and a few reach 1000 square metres in size.

This was an assize town where taxes and duties were levied. As such it became an important banking centre. Coins have been found around the Treasury which originated in scores of foreign countries, but were brought to Ephesus by pilgrims and traders. It was the seat of the Proconsul of Asia from 133 BC. The might of the Roman Army was obvious. Today a frieze of fully armed Roman soldiers complete with armour, helmet, sword, shield and sandals still stands where early Christians, passing the stadium, would remember how Paul reminded them to put on 'the whole armour of God' — including the breastplate, girdle and sandals — and to take up the helmet, sword and shield.

It was also a centre known for immorality. Ephesus was the sex capital of Asia. Even on the streets of Ephesus today we still see carved into the stonework the sign of a heart, a bare-breasted woman and an arrow pointing to one building along the Marble Way that was a brothel. Its intention is still as clear as the day it was first cut into the marble.

Paul had established the church in Ephesus during a two- to three-year ministry.[3] He was imprisoned here and caused a city-wide riot. When Paul wrote his first letter to the Corinthians from Ephesus, he sent greetings from Priscilla and Aquila, the husband and wife team of tent-maker evangelists. Paul had stayed with them in Corinth, working as a tent-maker alongside them following their expulsion from Rome with the other Jews under the Edict of Emperor Claudius in AD 49. They had then crossed from Corinth to Ephesus and supported Paul in the new church. Timothy also ministered here and in the hinterland and John had come to Ephesus from Jerusalem to minister to the people. Tradition says that John brought the aging Mary, mother of Jesus, with him, and she died in Ephesus. It was from here he wrote his great Gospel according to John.

How a British archeologist discovered the site and excavated Ephesus dispels the romanticism of archeology and demonstrates the hard work and commitment

Children in Ephesus today

required for the task.

The British Museum sent John Turtle Wood (what kind of parent would call a son, Turtle?) to the area where he was to work faithfully for the next eleven years. His training as an architect led him to make some calculated guesses as to where in the swamps the temple of Artemis might be and where, later, the great theatre might be found. For six years as he combatted malaria, thieves, derision and the Turkish government, Wood hammered long steel rods into the ground hoping to strike buried marble, but with no success. Then, during a winter when he was forced to work on higher ground, he discovered the great theatre where Paul had been dragged. Digging through centuries of accumulated rubble and dirt, he uncovered some inscriptions on the outside of the theatre, copies of letters sent from the Emperor Hadrian and, on the southern entrance, an account of a Roman's gift of gold and silver images of Artemis housed in the temple. He had lived in Ephesus only decades after Paul!

Soon afterwards, twenty feet below the surface, he reached the base of the greatest building of the ancient world! It took him another four years of labour to retreive the famous columns and to open to the world the site of the temple. Such is the life of an archeologist.

The letter to the church at Ephesus has four emphases.

Paul opens with the words of *praise*: 'I know what you have done; I know how hard you have worked and how patient you have been. . . You are patient, you have suffered for my sake, and you have not given up.' This was high praise for their works, their patience and their enduring of suffering. Paul had foretold that 'fierce wolves' would come among the flock of God after he had left them. But they had remained faithful.

Secondly, he observes a *problem*: 'this is what I have against you: you do not love me now as you did at first.' That church had lost their love for Jesus Christ, their faith had faded into mere form and they had lost the real power of their faith.

Thirdly, Paul orders a *procedure*: 'Think how far you have fallen! Turn from your sins and do what you did at first.' The answer to their problem was simple. They had to remember how far they had fallen, to repent of their sins, and to reaffirm the faith as they did at first. This threefold procedure is still of value for those who have turned away from their primary commitment to Jesus.

Finally, in the letter he offered them two *promises*. The first is: 'If you don't turn from your sins, I will come to you and take your lamp-stand from its place.' If there was no true repentance, then they would cease to be a church, their light would be taken from them and, if they didn't return to their first love, they would lose their gift of eternal life. That threat still remains for Christians today.

The second promise is to those who remain faithful: 'To those who win the victory I will give

the right to eat the fruit of the tree of life that grows in the Garden of God.' They would fulfil the destiny originally planned for Adam — to live in paradise and to eat of the tree of life. To have trees in a garden was the ancient idea from Persia — and every dry and barren land — of 'paradise'.[4]

Each one of us who lives in a strategic city of commercial and political significance, with religious and educational centres, libraries and brothels, needs to be reminded that Jesus knows where we live, he understands our situation and he calls us constantly back to our first love lest we lose the light of life.

The church at Smyrna
The second letter that John wrote was to the church at Smyrna. This church was thirty-five miles to the north of Ephesus. Today, Smyrna is the thriving city of Izmir, the third largest city of Turkey, with a population approaching one million.

At the time of John it was a magnificently planned city of well over 100,000 people, rebuilt on a planned basis after disastrous destruction in 580 BC. Her deep harbour never silted, and nearby are the ruins of the old forum. In earlier times a ring of palatial homes round Mount Pagus could be seen from afar.

The city of Smyrna was known among Christians for two things: first, it was the centre of Caesar worship and consequently opposition to the early Christians. In 195 BC the temple of Dea Roma was built, the first such temple to be built honouring Rome as a god. They quickly proved their loyalty to Rome by instituting Caesar worship. Christians refused to worship Caesar as Lord and so were persecuted for their faith. Second, it was a centre of opposition to the Christian faith by Jews. A holocaust occurred, Christians being persecuted by Jews whom Jesus described as not true Jews, otherwise they would not have acted that way. Archeologists, working under the difficulty of having a living city on top of the ancient one, have not been able to complete extensive digs in Izmir, and to date no reference to a Jewish community in the first century has been found.

To this church in Smyrna the message came by the hand of John writing from the island of Patmos: 'Do not be afraid, be faithful!' That theme of faithfulness under suffering was spelt out in the letter to the church at Smyrna in four ways.

Firstly, they were to be faithful in times of poverty. 'I know your troubles; I know that you are

poor — but really you are rich!' Most of the early Christians were poor and many of them had been plundered by their persecutors. The use of this word indicates they were completely destitute. But they were rich in heavenly blessings. Jesus knew their situation and supported them in it. In AD 105 just a few years after John wrote, St Ignatius, the third Bishop of Antioch on the Orontes, passed through Smyrna on his way to Rome, where he was martyred in the Colosseum. Later, on board ship, John wrote to commend them for their 'immovable faith as if nailed to the cross of the Lord Jesus Christ'.

Secondly, they were to be faithful in time of scorn. 'I know the evil things said against you by those who claim to be Jews but are not; they are a group that belongs to Satan!' How those early Christians suffered from slander and scorn. They were charged with cannibalism because it was said that they ate and drank the blood and body of Jesus. They were charged with incest because they called one another brother and sister.

Thirdly, they were encouraged to be faithful in times of imprisonment. 'Don't be afraid of anything you are about to suffer. Listen! The Devil will put you to the test by having some of you thrown into prison and your troubles will last ten days.' Their imprisonment was going to last long enough to hurt them, but short enough to eventually be concluded. Their endurance would be tested to the limit, but not beyond.

Fourthly, they were to be faithful in times of death. 'Be

faithful to me, even if it means death, and I will give you life as your prize of victory.'⁵ Jesus had promised his followers persecution and death and Peter had encouraged Christians to be faithful even to death. The cross was the symbol of their discipleship.

The faithful Christians in Smyrna were willing to face even death. Their crown was to be eternal life not hindered by the second death of judgment. This letter, like that to the church in Philadelphia, was one of unqualified praise.

Little did they know it, but not long afterwards, in AD 156, Polycarp, their beloved minister and bishop, was to be martyred by being burnt to death in the persecution. Yet his death inspired generations of Christians to come.

There were some games being held in Smyrna and wreaths of victory were being handed out to those who had won. The city was crowded with people from all the areas around. Someone in the crowd, wanting more excitement, called 'Away with the atheists — away with the traitors to the empire. Let Polycarp be searched for!' He was known for his strength of witness and for his leadership of the church. He was held in high regard by the city officials, but such was the pressure of the mob that the old man who had led the church following the death of John was dragged through the streets and brought before the magistrates. The police pleaded with him to say 'Caesar is Lord' and the magistrates begged that he acknowledge Rome as divine. But Polycarp refused.

The Proconsul begged him, 'Swear and I will release you; curse Christ!' and the old man, drawing himself up with straight back, said, 'Eighty and six years have I served him, and he has done me no wrong: how then can I blaspheme my King who saved me?' The crowd shouted to curse Christ or die. Polycarp elected to die. Very quickly dried branches were heaped into a bonfire around a huge stake. Ropes were brought to bind Polycarp, but he told them to take the ropes away: 'He who gives me power to endure the fire will grant me to remain in the flames.' The crowd shouted for the fire to be brought and Polycarp raised his arms to heaven and said, 'Oh Lord God Almighty, through whom we have received our knowledge of thee, I bless thee that thou hast deemed me worthy to this day and hour that I might take a portion among the martyrs in the cup of Christ to the resurrection to eternal life. May I today be welcome before thy face.' The fire burnt up brightly and those that were there insist that a wind blew the flames outward so that for some time he stood there in the midst not burning but shining like gold and a fragrance filled the theatre.

As John's revelation circulated around all the churches, each received a special message. To the church at Ephesus was the word of faithfulness, and to the church at Smyrna was the word of encouragement in time of suffering. This book strengthened Christians wherever it was read throughout the ancient world and is always read most and loved most by those who are suffering most.

For personal reading

Theme: The Lord of the churches I

MONDAY	Jesus appears to John *Revelation 1:9-18*
TUESDAY	The church is established at Ephesus *Acts 19:1-20*
WEDNESDAY	The message to the church at Ephesus *Revelation 2:1-7*
THURSDAY	How to test the spirits *1 John 4:1-6*
FRIDAY	Counteracting the teaching of the Nicolaitans *Romans 6:1-14*
SATURDAY	The message to the church at Smyrna *Revelation 2:8-11*
SUNDAY	How the believers are rich *James 2:1-13*

For group study

Topic: Jesus speaks to Ephesus and Smyrna

1 What is the purpose of the book of Revelation?

2 How was it greeted in the first century?

3 What do we learn about false teaching from 1 John 4 and Romans 6?

4 What can we learn from the letter to the church at Ephesus?

5 What can we learn from the letter to the church at Smyrna?

10

The Seven Churches: Pergamum and Thyatira

Our journey through the churches of first century Turkey takes us next to Pergamum and Thyatira.

Pergamum

The modern city of Bergama on the site of ancient Pergamum consists of a large flat plain in Anatolia dominated by a steep, thousand-foot-high mountain. From this vantage point, one can see the far ranges, the plains of Anatolia and the sea twenty-one kilometres away. This incredibly steep acropolis consists of high walls, several temples, a palace,

Ruins at Pergamum

library, three theatres and a great sacrificial altar to Zeus.

Unlike the Athenian acropolis which was entirely sacred in nature, Pergamum was a mixture of sacred and secular: temples and theatres, market places, arsenals, the palace and the gymnasium. The populace could mix and talk, buy and sell, worship and play sports in the one area on the top and precipitous side of the mountain. The city was safe from attack and provided a good defensive position for the surrounding countryside.

Early artifacts, similar to those found in Troy, indicate the area has been continuously inhabited since at least 800 BC. An early tomb of a princess became a famous temple for people from the Phrygian area. Xenophon and his ten thousand marauding Greek troops stayed here, conquering some of the surrounding countryside. Pergamum sided with Alexander the Great against the Persians in 334 BC. Under his successors, the acropolis was heavily fortified and became the centre of the Pergamum kingdom, which lasted until captured by the Romans following a twenty-seven-year war. Under the Romans the city spread down onto the plain

Fortifications at Pergamum

and reached a population of 150,000. In the Christian era, Arabs and Turks have successively occupied the area.

In 1878, teams of German archeologists commenced excavations of the acropolis and the various temples and theatres, removing much of the statuary to East Berlin, including the famous Altar of Zeus. German archeologists have worked hard to present to the world the wonderful city of Pergamum. As the visitor travels the site today — in parts a very demanding physical exercise! — he notices three areas: the acropolis, the town centre and the Asklepieum.

Pergamum was a cultural centre. There is a large theatre and two smaller ones, a cultural centre for theatre and arts, and the second largest library in the ancient world. Wide stoas surrounded the library, providing shelter for citizens. The two-storey library at Pergamum held 200,000 volumes and every shelf

was free-standing half-a-metre from the wall, thus protecting the volumes from damp. Rows of windows topped the walls. It was here the art of writing on skins known as parchment was developed and the very word 'parchment' developed from the words 'he pergamene charta' or 'the Pergamene sheet'. It was developed when the king of Pergamum, anxious that his library should outstrip the greatest library in the world, bribed the Alexandrian librarian to shift to Pergamum. But the librarian was imprisoned so he could not go, and the Ptolemy of Egypt banned the export of Egyptian papyri to Pergamum. The experts in Pergamum then developed a vellum from animal skins which was superior to papyri and which eventually replaced papyri altogether.

The palaces were the homes of the kings and luxurious in their fittings. Nearby are four arsenals including a good supply of rounded boulders from three kilos to seventy-five kilos in weight. These were fired down upon enemies and would have had an immediate effect in scattering the enemy!

Dominating the area were a number of temples to Athena, Dionysus, Hera Basileia, Asklepios, Hermes and Heracles. Crowning the area from the viewpoint of anyone approaching from the plain was an enormous temple to Zeus Soter. Most of this temple to Zeus was taken pillar by pillar and stone by stone to Germany by nineteenth-century archeologists where it has been re-erected in the Pergamum Museum in East Berlin. While most of the

The Acropolis at Pergamum

statuary is still in place, one battered marble giant, which had lain for two centuries in a council junk yard in Worksop, London, has been identified as once having been part of the frieze. To early Christians, this temple to 'Zeus the Saviour' would have been quickly identified as 'Satan's Throne'. The altar to Zeus Soter — the very word means 'saviour' — would have been seen by the Christians as being the very opposite to what they believed: Jesus Christ was the only Saviour. This temple stood on the highest point above the flat valley.

The central township consists of a number of temples, marketplaces, stoas, fountains, baths, gymnasia, shops, colonnades and the interests of the general public.

The temple of Asklepios was dedicated to the serpent god of

healing, also known as 'Saviour God'. This led down to the Asklepieum, one of the most important therapeutic centres in the ancient world. People came here for healing from the fourth century BC. The approach was along a sacred road nearly a kilometre long, lined with columns. Statues, fountains, a library, transparent alabaster windows and marble stairs made an imposing centre. A theatre seated 3,500, with a forty-seat men's toilet and a seventeen-seat (much plainer) women's toilet, and beautiful colonnades led to the hot water baths, cold water baths, mud baths, massage rooms and ointment rooms. One feature is the long eighty-metre tunnel which led to the centre of the Asklepieum. In this Asklepieum people, brought for treatment, would sleep the night and while still in the dark would walk

Tunnel at Pergamum

through this long tunnel where snakes would hiss at them and cold water and objects would be dropped upon them from the roof above. The psychological relief from fear at the end aided psychosomatic healing!

Pergamum was known as one of the centres for healing in the ancient world. It manufactured healing drugs and developed scientific methodology. This Asklepieum was so named because of the symbol of the snake around the pole — still used as a sign by medical doctors today. Galen, one of the greats of early medicine and the famous anatomist, practised in the Asklepieum. It was visited by Hippocrates, the father of medicine, from his birthplace on Cos, an island near Patmos. His Hippocratic Oath guides doctors all round the world even in the twentieth century. But the serpent, so central in Pergamum, would have a symbolism for the early Christian that was associated with Satan.

Confrontation between the Christian believers and the state religion and the medical practices of Pergamum was bound to occur. We do not know who founded the church in this city, but by the final third of the first century it was under the oversight of Bishop Gaius, the same man to whom John wrote the third epistle that bears his name. That little letter gives some guidance to Gaius for his leadership in the church, and warns about a rather terrible man by the name of Diotrephes who had done John a great hurt.

The successor to Gaius was Antipas who became the leader of the church and its first martyr. His name is perhaps symbolic, meaning that he stood for the faith against all or *anti pas*.

The letter
In the letter to the church at Pergamum, Jesus said: 'This is the message from the one who has the sharp two-edged sword. I know where you live, there where Satan has his throne.'[1] As mentioned earlier, the giant altar of Zeus Soter was probably known as the throne of Satan.

The letter has three messages in it.

Firstly, he says, 'You are true to me and you did not abandon your faith in me even during the time when Antipas, my faithful witness, was killed there where Satan lives.'[2] This was a word of *approval*. Here was a church that deserved to be praised because they were true to their Lord and refused to abandon their faith. Antipas was dragged before the proconsul of the area and an attempt was made to force him to say 'Caesar is Lord', but that to him was not possible. He would rather die than deny his Lord. Antipas, refusing to abandon his faith, died true to his Lord by being roasted alive within a bronze statue of a bull.

The others in the church were strengthened in their resolve to be faithful due to the courage of Antipas. Did you notice that Satan dwells where they lived? Satan's throne towered above the city and Satan's serpent was seen in their streets. The source of evil is never far from us. If love was essential for the church at Ephesus, then truth was its partner and the church at

Pergamum

Pergamum had stuck with the truth. They were 'true to me and you did not abandon your faith in me', says the Lord. The church must always stand for doctrinal truth and acknowledge Jesus Christ as the only Saviour in the face of Zeus, Asklepios and other modern 'saviours' of our world.

The second message, however, concerned some in the church who did not hold fast like Antipas. For them there is the word of *accusation*:

But there are a few things I have against you: there are some among you who follow the teachings of Balaam, who taught Balak how to lead the people of Israel into sin by persuading them to eat food that had been offered to idols and to practise sexual immorality. In the same way you have people among you who follow the teaching of the Nicolaitans.[3]

These Nicolaitans were some people in the local community who tried to get the church to compromise on its stand by accepting the influence of idol worship and by practising sexual immorality. Those who tempted the church were like the tempter Balaam who tried to seduce the Israelites into idolatrous and immoral conduct with some Moabite girls.[4] Christians are always under the temptation to compromise their behaviour from the high standards of Christ. But we are called not only to be true to him, but true to the standards of his faith. Correct belief must be accompanied by correct behaviour.

The final thing in the letter is a word of *admonition*. The challenge was: 'Now turn from your sins! If you don't I will come to you soon and fight against those people with the sword that comes out of my mouth.'[5] They, like the other churches throughout this area, were called upon to turn, to repent and to obey in order to have spiritual life.

And how does Christ fight against those who deny the faith and betray his standards? With the word of the Lord, the word of God — the Bible. So we are expected to use the sword of the Lord in keeping to the standards of Christ. Like the short, sharp Roman two-edged sword, so the Bible, in both the Old and the New Testament, cuts at our sins, pierces our pride, severs our dependency upon this world, lays bare our inadequacies and kills all that is wrong within.

The letter finishes with the usual admonition 'to listen to what the Spirit says to the churches!' and then adds 'To those who win the victory I will give some of the hidden manna. I will also give each of them a white stone on which is written a new name that no one knows except the one who received it.'[6]

The promise was for spiritual food that would sustain them. The heavenly manna, which was Christ himself come from heaven, was an invitation to be with him

in heaven free from guilt. The people of Pergamum would have seen a white stone taken by a judge who would cast it as a ballot of acquittal. They would have known of a name being written on a flat white stone as a ticket of admission to a great feast. Christians still sing, 'Write thy new name upon my heart, thy new best name of love.' Perhaps the Lord was reminding them of their acquittal from sin and of the great bridal feast of heaven to which they had been invited. The promise was of his abiding presence and the hope of heaven.

Thyatira
The person who delivered the letters, from the words of Jesus delivered to John on Patmos, wound his way up the great trade route that connected all seven churches. Having started in Ephesus, he had travelled north to Sardis and Pergamum. Now he turned south east and journeyed seventy kilometres to Thyatira.

Thyatira was the only one of the seven churches that was situated on flat land with absolutely no defences at all. It was a city of little strategic importance and possessed no political or cultural achievements in its history. Many times it had been overrun by invaders intent on capturing the wealthy city of Pergamum. For the previous two hundred years it had not even possessed its own coins.

But it was widely known for its commercial interests, especially its textile industry. There was a large woollen industry in the region and this was the home of a great industry in weaving and dyeing cloth. The rich, flat plains were ideal for raising both black sheep with their thick curly wool, and the fine goat-hair that still is the proud export from their area. And through their city traversed a significant trade route to Byzantium.

This was the home of Lydia whom Paul saw converted at Philippi in Macedonia. She was a seller of purple cloth highly prized by the Romans, and still used today by royalty and cardinals. Her business had stretched from Asia to Europe and evidently she was a wealthy woman. It is not surprising to read later that when Paul was in prison the church of which Lydia was a leader was very generous in sending financial support and goods to help Paul. In 1872, archeologists discovered in Philippi an inscription of gratitude to one Antiochus from Thyatira who was a dyer of purple cloth.

But the city of Thyatira had another feature. It hosted the movement of workers' guilds, which later in modern times developed into trade unions. The records tell us of unions of weavers, dyers, clothiers, bronze workers, bakers, cobblers, tanners, slave-dealers, linen workers, garment makers and potters: in fact, more different kinds of guilds have been revealed in Thyatira than in any other ancient city. Every workers' guild was attached to a temple and, in order to get work, it was necessary to make sacrifices to idols. It was simply a matter of being economically viable by not being so particular about their faith commitment. This was the old problem faced by the Corinthians who had to share the idols' meat if they were going to have permission to work at their trade.

The early Christians who refused to do this were therefore refused permission by the unions to participate in any work and therefore earn their living. They were persecuted greatly because they were faithful in their belief and insisted upon holiness of living.

The letter
The longest of the seven letters was sent to the church in the smallest town. But their faith had been severely compromised. Wherever the guilds were strong — and they were nowhere as strong as in Thyatira — immorality and idolatry were rife.

John had four things to say to this church. The letter starts with *approval*. Jesus reveals how much he knows about the church in the city to which he sent the letter when he says, 'This is the message from the Son of God, whose eyes blaze like fire, whose feet shine like polished brass'.[7] This is the only use of this expression 'polished brass' in the New Testament and comes directly from the guild of brass burnishers. Those people in Thyatira were famous for polished brass throughout the ancient world.

This is the only time in the Book of Revelation that Jesus claims to be the Son of God. That claim is deliberate, for in Thyatira there was a significant temple to Apollo, the Sun God.

Jesus says, 'I know what you do. I know your love, your faithfulness, your service, and your patience. I know that you are doing more now than you did

at first.'[8] Incredible as it seems to those who know what their church life was really like, those Christians in Thyatira had the love that Ephesus lacked, they were faithful to their doctrine which was under threat in Pergamum, their service was equal to that at Ephesus, and their patience was like that in Sardis.

But further: Ephesus was losing her first love, yet Thyatira was doing more now than she ever had done for the sake of Christ. She was practising church growth principles! He approves their loyalty and service. What a tremendous message of praise to a church whose love, faithfulness and service were even greater now than they were in earlier days.

Secondly, there is *accusation*: 'But this is what I have against you: you tolerate that woman Jezebel, who calls herself a messenger of God. By her teaching she misleads my servants into practising sexual immorality and eating food that has been offered to idols.' Jezebel again! We first met her in the Old Testament where she tried to seduce the priests of God. Now in Thyatira there was another one of her kind. Indeed, every generation has its quota of seductive women who try to adulterate the faith by their immoral practices. In every great city of the world today, there are still those who deny their faith by not disciplining their sex lives.

The name is symbolic of some person who acted like the original Jezebel. She married Ahab and brought the worship of Baal alongside Jehovah. She did not try to remove the worship of the one true God, but simply tried to dilute it by adding her own god. She seduced believers into lowering their standards, in compromising their faith on the matters of idolatry and immorality, in order that they might keep their jobs. The church was tolerating evil in their midst. Jesus says he had 'given her time to repent of her sins, but she does not want to turn from her immorality'.[10] What an accusation!

Thirdly, there is a word of warning, of *admonition*: 'And so I will throw her onto a bed where she and those who committed adultery with her will suffer terribly. I will do this now unless they repent of the wicked things they did with her. I will also kill her followers.'[11] That severe warning to repent lest they be terribly punished must have caused the Christians in this centre to sit up and take notice! That letter would have had a powerful effect as it admonished their sinfulness.

Finally, the letter closes with a promise that repentance would bring them a new *authority*:

But the rest of you in Thyatira have not followed this evil teaching; you have not learnt what the others call 'the deep secrets of Satan' . . . until I come, you must continue to the end to do what I want. To those who win the victory . . . I will give them the same authority that I received from my Father: I will give them authority over the nations . . . I will also give them the morning star.[12]

Here was a promise to them: that if they remained true and faithful, they would have God's authority upon them and the presence of the one who was called 'the bright and morning star', Jesus himself. The symbolism of the morning star lies in its apparent immortality. Authority and immortality — what great gifts!

God's call to repentance is not only for sinful people who are disobedient to his commands, but to church members who have lowered their standards. We must all hear 'what the Spirit says to the churches'. In a world where compromise is common, the letters to the churches at Pergamum and Thyatira have a great relevance to us today. Libertinism is always a threat to the purity of the gospel and to the holiness of a Christian life. Christians are called to live a distinctive lifestyle. 'The unrighteous will not inherit the kingdom of God,' said Paul bluntly.

In every major city of the world, Christians are being called to moral and spiritual compromise by those people who would easily deny faith. They may dress up their proposals to sound reasonable and modern, but the new moralities are just the old immoralities in a new dress. But the church is not called to be well-adjusted to a society that is going to hell. The church is not called to conform to the standards of this world. Christians today are called to march to the beat of a different drum. We are called not to be trendy, but to be trans-formed into the image of Christ.

For personal reading

Theme: The Lord of the churches I

MONDAY
: The message to the church at Pergamum
Revelation 2:12-17

TUESDAY
: The teaching of Balaam
Numbers 24:14; 32:15-16

WEDNESDAY
: The lawless one
2 Thessalonians 2:1-12

THURSDAY
: The church at Thyatira
Revelation 2:18-29

FRIDAY
: The prophetess Jezebel
1 Kings 16:29-34

SATURDAY
: Jezebel's punishment
1 Kings 21:17-26

SUNDAY
: God the potter
Jeremiah 18:1-12

For group study

Topic: Jesus speaks to Pergamum and Thyatira

1 The church at Pergamum was in the midst of idolatry and immorality. What was the teaching of Balaam that John's letter refers to? (See Tuesday's personal reading.)

2 How can this be a problem for the church today?

3 The church at Thyatira was in the midst of material wealth. What warnings were given to the church there?

4 The Western church today is part of a materialistic culture. How can the teaching in the letter of Thyatira help us?

5 How is the picture of God in Jeremiah 18:1-12 relevant to us?

11

The Seven Churches: Sardis, Philadelphia, Laodicea

The final three churches on our tour of first century Turkish cities are found at Sardis, Philadelphia and Laodicea.

Sardis

Croesus was King of Sardis in Turkey. To be 'as rich as Croesus' was a saying in the ancient world because he was legendary for the gold and wealth that he had accumulated. When Croesus consulted the oracle at Delphi in Greece, he sent many gifts, including a pure gold lion weighing 250 kilos set on a pyramid of 117 blocks of gold and silver.

Croesus wanted to embark upon a war with Cyrus King of Persia, but before he launched his massive attack against Cyrus he first of all went to the Delphic oracle. The oracle was available on the seventh day of each month. Croesus asked the oracle if he would be successful. The enigmatic oracle replied, 'If Croesus crosses the River Halys, a great empire will be destroyed.' He did and it was. He crossed the River Halys between Lydia and Persia with a great army and he destroyed a great empire — his own! Defeated, Croesus fled back to Sardis and locked himself inside his impregnable city. He felt safe and secure on the great mountain upon which the city stood. The Persians, finding a way up, entered through the walls and found — no guards on duty! Sardis was asleep, safe in its own security! Cyrus and his soldiers let in the other members of his army and the city was captured while it was asleep.

Sardis lies about thirty-five miles southeast of Thyatira and fifty miles due east of Smyrna. The city is at the junction of the highways leading to these cities and to Pergamum. It was not only the home of Croesus, but in time was the headquarters of Alexander the Great and Antiochus the Great. In AD 17 it was devastated by an earthquake and with the help of Emperor Tiberius was rebuilt into a great city.

Sardis was the centre of a very strong Jewish community dating back at least four centuries before Christ. The number of Jews in the city increased dramatically and some of these were involved in the development of the first church. In 1962 a huge synagogue with a beautiful mosaic floor was discovered alongside the main Ismir-Ankara road through Sardis dating from the second century AD. This synagogue had the capacity of containing several thousand worshippers. It contained several well-preserved Jewish carvings and synagogue decorations, including seven branched candlesticks or menorah, trumpets, lions, palms and seals — all spoken of in John's Revelation.

Next to it lies a large gymnasium and a colonnade which lies under the highway. The gymnasium was an offence to the Jews, for the men competed naked and Jewish circumcision was exposed to ridicule. Remains of non-kosher food, including pigs, have been found in this area, confirming the offences to the Jews.

In Sardis today, there are the remains of the Temple of Artemis which was never finished before being turned into a centre for Christian worship, and nearby, the remains of a brick church from the fifth century. Two other nearby churches date from the fourth century. In 1958, archeologists discovered several important Christian relics, including a portrait of the apostle John from the third century.

Each of the other surrounding churches regarded Sardis highly for its vitality. There were no

Ruins at Sardis

false teachers and no suggestions of a Jezebel, a Balaam or the Nicolaitans. Yet it had an inner disease.

The church was established in Sardis by Clement, one of the young ministers sent by Paul to help establish churches in centres away from where Paul himself visited. The church grew well in its early days, but then under the pressures of persecution became quiet — in fact, so quiet that it was asleep. It was the first church of nominal Christians.

The apostle John wrote to the church in Sardis that it should wake up lest it suffer the same fate as did its city: outward vitality but inward decay. The letter to them started sternly: 'This is the message from the one who has the seven spirits of God and the seven stars. I know what you are doing; I know that you have the reputation for being alive, even though you are dead.'[1]

First, John's letter offers a *reassurance* that Jesus holds the churches — the seven stars — and their pastors safely in his hands. But who are 'the seven spirits of God'? They are the Holy Spirit, mentioned in Revelation 1:4 where the seven spirits are linked with the Father and the Son as the source of grace and peace. He refers to the Spirit's seven-fold energies being available for each of the seven churches.

Second, it offers a *rebuke*. Once more Jesus was able to say, 'I know. . . I know. . .' He understood the situation the church was in and was able to rebuke them for their lack of persistence and faithfulness. They were a church like many today who were living on their history.

It was full of nominal Christians. They had a reputation for being alive, even though they were dead. Many contemporary churches have started well and have had a great history of programs and witness, but in fact are now dead, living on their past reputation and history. Churches like this need a rebuke from Jesus to wake them up.

This is a reminder of Jesus' criticism of the internally dead. 'How terrible for you, teachers of the Law and Pharisees! You hypocrites! You are like whitewashed tombs, which look fine on the outside but are full of bones and decaying corpses on the inside. In the same way, on the outside you appear good to everybody, but inside you are full of hypocrisy and sins.'[2]

Third, John's letter offers the following *remedy*: 'So wake up, and strengthen what you have before it dies completely. For I find that what you have done is not yet perfect in the sight of my God. Remember, then, what you were taught and what you heard;

obey it and turn from your sins.'³

This instruction to wake up is a reminder of Jesus' words in John's Gospel where he says: 'I am telling you the truth: the time is coming — the time has already come — when the dead will hear the voice of the Son of God, and those who hear it will come to life.'⁴ In every generation, many hear the voice of God's Son and wake from spiritual death. They must then strengthen their own spiritual lives. This word 'strengthen' was a favourite word among the New Testament pastors: Paul, Peter, James and others use the word to instruct the new Christians to build themselves up in their faith. Many churches have spiritual reserves that are untouched and resources that are not exercised. So Jesus calls the church to strengthen what it already has because, if it does not do so, it dies. They must then obey the command to be the church, repenting of their sin. Obedience and repentance are two daily steps for the Christians to develop a life of discipleship. If they failed in carrying out the remedy for revival that Jesus proposed, Jesus said: 'I will come upon you like a thief and you will not even know the time when I will come.'⁵

Jesus warned the members in Ephesus that he would come and remove their lampstand if they did not repent; he warned the church at Pergamum that he would come with the sword of the Spirit; and now he warns the church at Sardis he will come unexpectedly in judgment if they do not quickly respond.

Fourth, Jesus in John's letter offers them a *reward*: 'A few of

you there in Sardis have kept your clothes clean. You will walk with me, clothed in white, because you are worthy to do so. Those who win the victory will be clothed like this in white, and I will not remove their names from the book of the living.'⁶ Here was the promise that those who kept themselves pure and faithful as they were when they first wore their white baptismal robes would walk with Jesus with their names written in God's book of life.

The names in the book of life were frequently mentioned in Revelation and also in the rest of the New Testament. Clothed in white, they would join the Messianic procession following the rider on the white horse.⁷ The poor, ill-clad American Negro comforted himself by thinking of that day in heaven, saying: 'I got a robe, you got a robe, all God's children got a robe!'

The life of purity and faithfulness does have its own inherent reward. The Christian is promised the presence of Christ, the gift of eternal life and a future in heaven. The Christian can sing with confidence: 'When the roll is called up yonder — I'll be there!' That reward lies ahead for the faithful. Let me ask you: Does your church have a reputation for being alive while it is in fact spiritually dead? Well, wake up to yourselves, strengthen what you have before it dies completely, repent and obey Jesus' word — a word not only to churches of the first century but to the twentieth as well.

Philadelphia

Over three hundred years ago, in 1681, King Charles II gave William Penn a charter to establish a new colony in North America, to be known as Pennsylvania. This colony was founded on the twin hopes of providing a new environment of religious freedom and a new opportunity for economic growth. The capital was to reflect these hopes and so was named Philadelphia. In time, Philadelphia was to become one of America's great cities. It was named after the town in Turkey that received the sixth letter from John on Patmos. This church at Philadelphia has, of all cities, the most beautiful name: it means 'the city of brotherly love'.

The town and church were set in a valley which was the gateway to the central plateau of Turkey. The city was the gateway to the centre of Turkey. King Attalus the Second of Pergamum, founded this colony of Philadelphia as an opportunity for spreading the Greek culture further into Lydia and Phrygia.

It was a fierce volcanic area known in Greek as *katakekaumene* — the very word itself was enough to strike fear in the hearts of people living in this earthquake-prone volcanic region. Early writers like Strabo claimed that the persistent earthquakes cracked the walls of houses and caused the people to live with insecurity and great fear.

Today, little remains of the city of the first century when John wrote this letter, and the modern town of Alasehir covers what remains. For a thousand years under Islam a thousand or so Christians kept the faith in Philadelphia when all other cities became Muslim.

The church was small and of little power. It was established by Lucius, a kinsman of the apostle Paul, who appointed him to this area through which he had travelled. Later, Demetrius from Ephesus was appointed pastor by John the apostle. Demetrius became the first bishop of the church.

Its membership was faithful and it suffered, not from internal infidelity or sleepiness, but because of external persecution. Like Smyrna, it is not blamed for heresy or lack of spiritual effort, but rather it is praised for its resistance to Jews who persecuted them and, like the church at Smyrna, it was promised a crown.

John has Jesus saying to this church:

This is the message from the one who is holy and true. He has the key that belonged to David, and when he opens a door, no one can close it, and when he closes it, no one can open it. I know what you do; I know that you have a little power; you have followed my teaching and have been faithful to me. I have opened a door in front of you, which no-one can close.[8]

That faithful church had an opportunity to witness to the community. They were to be like the early founders of the city who came in a missionary endeavour to spread Greek culture, except this church had the opportunity to spread the true faith.

'An open door' was frequently used to describe a missionary opportunity which God was opening for the believers. Paul testified to the open doors of witness God opened for him on numerous occasions. In Rome, Ephesus and Philadelphia God had opened the door, even in the face of opposition. When God opens that door no person can shut it.

John goes on to quote Jesus as saying: 'Listen! As for that group that belongs to Satan, those liars who claim they are Jews but are not, I will make them come and bow down at your feet. They will all know that I love you.'[9] Many times the scriptures affirm that those who oppose the Messiah and his people are not true Jews, but are agents of Satan. Christians are the true Jews because they acknowledge the Messiah, and all others will one

Hierapolis

day acknowledge the church as the people of God.

'Because you have kept my command to endure, I will also keep you safe from the time of trouble which is coming upon the world to test all the people on earth. I am coming soon. Keep safe what you have, so that no-one will rob you of your victory prize.'[10] That church had to be faithful in time of difficulty and persecution and they were given the hope that Jesus will soon return. That promise, 'I am coming soon', gave great encouragement to the hearts of all Christians who read this letter during their time of persecution, and still encourages them to this day.

As with the other letters, Jesus not only praised the church but gave them the promise: 'I will make him who is victorious a pillar in the temple of my God, and he will never leave it. I will write on him the name of my God and the name of the city of my God, the new Jerusalem, which will come down out of

heaven from my God. I will also write on him my new name.'[11] The citizens of Philadelphia knew what it was like to be part of a new city, with beautiful temples and possessing a new name. In a spiritual sense, that promise still abides for those churches who realise that before them God opens the door of opportunity. The second Jerusalem is a spiritual community, and the faithful Philadelphians would be an unshakeable pillar in the temple where no earthquake would cause them to tremble.

The Christ who holds these angels of the churches in his hand, and who walks among them, is holy and true. That means that Jesus Christ has an intimate relationship with God and is utterly reliable.

It is he who has the keys of David, a Messianic figure who attributes to Jesus the authority to open heaven to those who believe. He holds the keys to death and the world of the dead, and has all authority on earth and in heaven. It is he who holds the key to salvation and to heaven's door. Now he has set before the believer an open door to the sanctuary of God's presence.[12]

Just as the city had been given the new name of Neocaesarea by Tiberius only decades before, so the Christian is part of a new temple in a new city possessing a new name. We have been promised to dwell with God in heaven. We are promised that we will be citizens in the new Jerusalem. Then we will also wear the name of Christ, the Lord of Lords. What of your church? Is God giving you an open door of opportunity demanding from you

faithfulness in your commitment to him?

Laodicea

The seventh church to receive the message from Jesus written by the apostle John was the church at Laodicea.

Today, at the junction of the Lycus and Maeander valleys, the outline of the once proud and wealthy city can easily be seen by the visitor. Great mounds of earth, the accumulation of the centuries, cover what were once noble buildings, and sheep quietly graze round the ruins of long aqueducts. Cotton is picked by Turkish women in the fields that cover what were once broad plazas and market places, and the railway from Smyrna to Denizli runs on top of what was once the main road.

The gymnasium, Odeon, stadium, two theatres, temple and aqueduct are visible but unrestored. Apart from the city gate, the aqueduct and part of the city wall, nothing has been excavated.

Laodicea was one of the largest cities in the entire empire by the first century BC. It was named after the wife of Antiochus the Great between 261 and 253 BC. The Emperor Hadrian visited the city in AD 29. By the second century AD, the city was calling itself 'the Metropolis of Asia'. It was a very wealthy city, the centre of banking and of goldsmithing for the whole region.

Around the wealthy Lycus Valley there were herds of famous black sheep whose raven-black wool was sought after for fine garments. This led to the development of a large textile industry which produced tunics known as trimita. This area was also known for its famous medical school that specialised in the treatment of ear and eye diseases.

The churches of Colossae, Laodicea, Hierapolis and other places were once powerful centres of Christian faith. Today they remain huge mounds waiting for the archeologists. One day they will be opened for the tourist as has the nearby ancient city of Aphrodisias.

The church was founded by Epaphras from nearby Colossae. One of the few surviving names from the first or second century in Laodicea is that of one Epaphras, recorded on a marble block. Could it perhaps be the same person who founded the church? The church met in the house of Nympha and for a while we know that Archippus ministered here, for Paul wrote, 'You are to read the letter the brothers in Laodicea will send you. And tell Archippus, "Be sure to finish the task you were given in the Lord's service'."[13]

Laodicea

How we wish we knew which letter that was, if somewhere some of it remains, and what the task was that Archippus had to complete. By the time of John's letter to the church, Archippus was no longer the minister. However, the letter referred to may be our Letter to the Ephesians.

It is possibly here or at nearby Colossae that Philemon lived, that wealthy slave-owning Christian to whom Paul sent his brief epistle in our New Testament. Archeologists discovered in this city of Laodicea a marble inscription which mentions the name of a prominent citizen named Marcus Sestius Philemon. Could this be the very Philemon to whom Paul wrote?

The letter of Jesus recorded by John to the church at Laodicea starts by affirming the nature of Jesus, the author: 'This is the message of the Amen the faithful and true witness, who is the origin of all that God created.'[14] Jesus himself emphasises the insights given by John and Paul that he was the one who was God's agent, the very originator of creation.

This letter has four parts.

In the first part, Jesus confronts the church which was as lukewarm as the water in the springs nearby. 'I know what you have done; I know that you are neither cold nor hot. How I wish you were either one or the other! But because you are lukewarm, neither hot nor cold, I am going to spit you out of my mouth!'[15]

He knew those lukewarm members and they made him sick. They reflected their affluent, self-centred, lukewarm environment. The church had no vitality and

Laodicea's lukewarm springs

enthusiasm within it. The early Christians in most places were enthusiasts for their faith. They went preaching the gospel, telling all they met in carriages, boats, shops or on footpaths; teaching, arguing, discussing, announcing, debating, gossiping, chattering, testifying the gospel. . . but not at Laodicea.

They were not opposed to the message, but they were not enthusiastic for it either. They preferred to be thought respectable rather than religious. They were lukewarm and Jesus said, 'I am going to spit you out of my mouth!' Here was a church that did not have a heart that 'burned within' from the presence of Jesus.

At every period of the church's growth, it has been led by faithful men and women who were enthusiastic for the gospel. John Wesley, for example, rode 250,000 miles on horseback, preached 40,000 sermons and wrote 200 books to help people grow in their faith. One charge brought against him and his early helpers was that he suffered from 'enthusiasm — a very dreadful condition'. In the deadness and dryness of the church of his century, those early Methodists brought revival. It is little wonder that the world is unimpressed with the message of the church when it notes the lack of spiritual passion among its members. Does your church recognise itself as a church that is neither hot nor cold? Jesus Christ does not like a lukewarm church.

The second part of this letter confronted them on their self-sufficient attitude. 'You say, "I am rich and well off; I have all I need." But you do not know how miserable and pitiful you are! You are poor, naked and blind.'[16]

Even in a city of wealth they were poor; in a city famous for its fine clothing industry they were naked; and in a city famous for its medical school specialising in eye healing, they were blind. The church is always in danger when it becomes self-sufficient, boasting of its buildings, programmes and pastors. That church does not even realise its own poverty in things of the Spirit, its own transparent nakedness in the eyes of God, its own wretchedness.

They were saying, 'I am rich... I have all...' but Jesus was calling them to see that their salvation was not of themselves, but was from him. He was the source of their inner satisfaction. Jesus had said, 'You can do nothing without me',[17] but this church was proud of what it could do on its own. Every

church has to beware of self-sufficiency and to see its own real condition.

But Jesus did not merely criticise; in the third part of this letter he counselled them to wholehearted commitment:

I advise you, then, to buy gold from me, pure gold, in order to be rich. Buy also white clothing to dress yourself and cover up your shameful nakedness. Buy also some ointment to put on your eyes so that you may see. I rebuke and punish all whom I love. Be in earnest, then, and turn from your sins.[18]

Smyrna thought itself poor when it was in fact rich; Laodicea thought itself rich when it was in fact poor. The Laodiceans could purchase from the *agora* many fine black tunics, but their nakedness needed to be covered by the white robes of righteousness and purity that only Jesus could provide. Those garments are heavenly. The tunics of Laodicea were earthly.

One grammatical point is of interest: Jesus uses the same word for the application of the eye ointment or salve as does the famous physician Galen, who described the ointment in his discussion on what he called Phrygian powders.

Jesus was the answer to their need. The Christians were told to come to him and find in him riches, clothing and healing. Always the church that is self-sufficient needs to come close to its Master and find from him the answers to their condition.

In the fourth part of the letter Jesus commands personal renewal.

Jesus says he rebukes and punishes those he loves. He still loves them and allows them to be refined through trials so they can become the people he wants them to be.

Jesus exhorts them to be in earnest and turn from their sins. Repentance is a single act of turning, but being in earnest is a continuous attitude. Those Christians needed to repent and to humble themselves before God and then recommit themselves to fervent faith in the same way as God has called his people in all generations.

Jesus concludes with an invitation that is one of the loveliest invitations of the entire Bible:

Listen! I stand at the door and knock; if anyone hears my voice and opens the door, I will come into his house and eat with him, and he will eat with me. To those who win the victory I will give the right to sit beside me upon my throne, just as I have been victorious and now sit by my Father on his throne.[19]

That invitation is addressed to any individual who hears his call. Even one person is able to respond. His promise is one of personal intimacy and closeness. Jesus graciously calls all of us who are poor, naked and blind to come to him. He stands before us at our heart's door and knocks, waiting for us to let him come in. And when he enters, our dining room becomes his throne room!

I stood in St Paul's Cathedral London and, as I walked out the aisle, I passed a great column

where Holman Hunt's well-known painting, *Jesus Christ, the Light of the World*, is hung. The picture is of a dark night and brambles cover a house, but Jesus the King is standing outside knocking on the door and the light from his lantern shines upon his kind face. He patiently waits for the door to be opened. There is no handle on the outside of the door: This door can only be opened from the inside! Jesus quietly says that he stands at the door and knocks. Each one of us has the opportunity of inviting him into our lives, our hearts, and our homes. Have you?

So, in the Spirit of Jesus, John wrote those seven letters to the seven churches in Turkey. He was writing them to those places at that time, but there is about those letters something that transcends time and place. They have been written to any church anywhere. As you hear the words of Jesus, may the Spirit of God himself give you ears to hear what the Spirit says to the churches.

For personal reading

Theme: The Lord of the churches III

MONDAY
The message to the church at Sardis
Revelation 3:1-6

TUESDAY
What the Pharisees are like
Matthew 23:27-28

WEDNESDAY
The suddenness of the Lord's coming
1 Thessalonians 5:1-11

THURSDAY
The message to the church at Philadelphia
Revelation 3:7-13

FRIDAY
Paul's open doors
Acts 14:27; 1 Corinthians 16:9;
2 Corinthians 2:12; Colossians 4:3-4

SATURDAY
The message of the church at Laodicea
Revelation 3:14-22

SUNDAY
The presence of the Lord within
Luke 24:32; Romans 12:9-21

For group study

Topic: Jesus speaks to Sardis, Philadelphia and Laodicea

1   How does Tuesday's reading throw light on the church at Sardis?

2   Do you ever wonder if the church is asleep? What can you do?

3   The church at Philadelphia clearly had an opportunity. What opportunities has God placed before you and your church? What are you doing about them?

4   How is the message to Laodicea a message of hope to us all?

5   What does Sunday's reading tell us about the nature of true church life?

12

The Revelation of John

The long water tunnel at Megiddo, visited today by many tourists, was dug by the engineers of King Solomon and completed some time in the reign of King Ahab around 800 BC. For four hundred feet it carried a strong water supply beneath a hill into the bottom of a large well in the heart of the city. This water supply enabled the city to become one of the strongest fortresses of the ancient world.

The first city of Megiddo was built in 3,500 BC and more than twenty cities have been built in this same spot one on top of the other. King Solomon used this city as his headquarters and his grain stores base. This fortified city held a commanding position

in north central Israel. Whoever held this garrison held the great plain of Esdraelon below.

This huge plain in Israel was frequently the battleground of mighty armies. It is the pivotal point between the continents of Asia, Africa and Europe. Over the years many great battles were fought: pharaohs led their Egyptians against Babylonians and Assyrians; Hittites against Egyptians and Assyrians; Canaanites against Israelites; Phoenicians against Philistines; Persians against Greeks and Parthians against Romans; Byzantines against Arabs; Crusaders against Turks; the British against Turks; and Jordanians against Israelis. Conquerors have made this the key to their winning the area from Pharaoh Thutmose III in 1468 BC right through to General Allenby in World War I. Allenby became known as Allenby, Viscount of Megiddo, 3,386 years after the first pharaoh passed by.

But battles of the past are of interest because the last book of the Bible says the last great battle on earth shall be fought at Megiddo, also known at Mt Megiddo, which in Hebrew is Har-Mageddon or Armageddon.

Why is this battle to be fought? Will the superpowers of this world clash over tension sparked by trouble in the Middle East? The Book of Revelation in its outline of a vision of the end of time claims the world will end in a holocaust commencing here.

The vision of the end

Somewhere between AD 90 and 95 , in a cave on the island of Patmos, the apostle John wrote the last book of the Bible, the Revelation of John. He records the vision that he had of the resurrected Jesus at a time when Christians were suffering from persecution in many parts of the world, a persecution that had exiled him as an old man to hard labour on this island.

After writing to the seven churches in Turkey, the rest of the book is a series of visions presented in symbolic language, understood by the Christians of his day but not by their persecutors. The information was passed on by word of mouth. Unfortunately, no-one today so completely understands the code involved in the series of visions that he is able to say with certainty what John intended in a few very obscure passages.

The Greek title of the book reveals its nature: *apokalypsis* means the uncovering of something that is revealed or hidden. He intended to make known to believers the hidden secrets of the future, and of Jesus Christ who is both the One who makes the revealing and who is the object of the revealing.

John presented God's great plan for mankind, and how the disrupting effects of Satan and his minions on earth will eventually be unable to disrupt the plan of God. That is why this book is so optimistic. Despite the worst that humankind can do, it tells of the ultimate triumph of God and those who believe in him. It gave great encouragement to those who were suffering from vile persecutions under the Romans, and ever since it has been loved most by those who suffer most.

The purpose of the book is revealed in its opening:

This book is the record of the events that Jesus Christ revealed. God gave him this revelation in order to show his servants what must happen very soon. Christ made these things known to his servant John by sending his angel to him, and John has told all that he has seen. This is his report concerning the message from God and the truth revealed by Jesus Christ. Happy is the one who reads this book, and happy are those who listen to the words of this prophetic message and obey what is written in this book! For the time is near when all these things will happen.[1]

Like the themes of a symphony, there is a weaving in and out and a repeating of the various series of visions. A number of symbols are repeated including the letters to the seven churches, the seven seals on the book, the seven trumpets, the seven signs, and the seven last plagues, until it reaches a great climax when Christ conquers all his enemies, including Satan, and brings to his persecuted followers a new heaven and a new earth.

Right at the beginning John establishes the message as coming from Jesus, who is called 'the faithful witness'.[2] But Jesus is not just the subject of the book; he is the object of it. The book leads

into the worship of Christ and is filled with pictures of believers worshipping Christ.[3] The tone of worship is set in these early verses:

He loves us, and by his death he has freed us from our sins and made us a kingdom of priests to serve his God and Father. To Jesus Christ be the glory and power forever and ever! Amen.
Look, he is coming on the clouds! Everyone will see him, including those who pierced him. All peoples on earth will mourn over him. So shall it be.[4]

A new type of writing

When John wrote Revelation, it was against a background of persecution. Two hundred years earlier, Jews under persecution had developed a new type of writing called *apocalyptic* literature. This is a form of writing that is unique, colourful and full of bright imagery. It is poetry, artistry and music rather than a scientific treatise of how great events would happen. It is a cartoonist's treatment of the events of the future rather than a bus timetable of when future events would occur.

To read it in the light of literalism is to miss the spirit of it. John's writings were designed to lift the hearts of the believers and leave them with a feeling of ultimate vindication and triumph over wrong. Similar passages of apocalyptic writing can be found in the Book of Daniel, especially in the chapters relating to the great image in the dream of King Nebuchadnezzar (chapter 2) and the multi-horned beasts (chapters 7 and 8) and the presentation of Daniel's seventy weeks. These passages were written only a couple of hundred years before the Revelation of John, and would have influenced him greatly.

A knowledge of the Old Testament greatly helps the reader in interpreting the message, for over three hundred references to the Old Testament are included in the book. This is one reason non-believers have great difficulty in understanding it.

The Revelation of John has been the happy hunting ground for religious fanatics, for people who want timetables to the future, and who like to chart the course of nations and dictators. It is little wonder that John sternly rebuked such in saying:

I, John, solemnly warn everyone who hears the prophetic words of this book: if anyone adds anything to them, God will add to his punishment the plagues described in this book. And if anyone takes away anything away from the prophetic words of this book, God will take away from him his share of the fruit of the tree of life and of the Holy City, which are described in this book.[5]

For this book is more than a mystery puzzle: it is a book that reaches to the spirit of persecuted people and gives them hope!

The Christians of the first two centuries were persecuted under a series of Roman emperors. The emperors walked through the Forum in the heart of the capital of the empire little considering the sufferings of the Christians on the fringes of the empire. But some suffered under the direct whim of the Emperor. Nero, for example,

The Roman Forum

instigated an incredible persecution following the disastrous fire of Rome in AD 64. During his persecution both Peter and Paul were murdered, and thousands of believers died as spectacles before the crowds. Nero was followed by Vespasian who, after re-establishing some stability throughout the empire, died in AD 79.

He was succeeded by his son Titus who reigned only two years. He was popular and was called the 'darling of the human race'. In the heart of ancient Rome stood the Forum, and dominating it leading to the Colosseum is the Arch of Titus. This arch recounts the triumph of General Titus in conquering the eastern part of the Roman Empire and shows slaves being dragged back to Rome to work on building the Colosseum. Among them is a group of Jews who are carrying their seven-branched candlestick, the menorah, as an indication that they are bringing their faith with them. Many Christians were also captured as slaves under Titus.

His younger brother, Domitian, then became Emperor. He called himself 'Lord and God'. He was a morose and suspicious man and saw Christians as atheists for they worshipped no visible idols. Because they gathered in secret, he suspected them of having much to hide and because they would

Enslaved Jews enter Rome
The Arch of Titus, Rome

not take part in the social events in the temples and in the immoralities of the day, he regarded them as pernicious. It was during his reign of terror that John was taken into exile in Patmos. Domitian was assassinated in AD 96.

He was followed for the next twenty years by the Emperor Trajan, who was suspicious of the young church and who ordered the early Christians to be executed if they did not abandon their faith. Later emperors continued the persecution up until the conversion of Constantine in AD 312.

During the persecution of Christians, many hid in catacombs beneath Rome. There are more than forty of these series of long tunnels, covering 800 kilometres in length. They are important to us as a source of the early faith of Christians who painted their pictures on the sides of the tombs and wrote their statements of faith. It was here they found shelter and met in refuge from a hostile world.

The Christians of the persecution, encouraged by John's vision of a future victory and the teaching of Jesus about immortal life, wrote on the sides of their graves slogans that have encouraged and inspired generations. We read on one, 'He sleeps and lives in the peace of Christ'; on another, 'The soul lives not knowing death and right consciously rejoices in the vision of Christ'; and on another, 'Thou livest in the glory of God and in the peace of Christ our Lord'.

The Christian doctrine of resurrection and victory is mentioned frequently, as in the following: 'Here rests my flesh; but at the last day, through Christ, I believe it shall be raised from the dead,' and, 'I believe, because my Redeemer lives, in the last day he shall raise me from the earth, and in my flesh I shall see the Lord.'

It is a moving experience to read these testimonies of faith and to walk through the catacombs. Those Christians who died in faith looked forward in hope to when they would share eternal life and victory with Jesus.

The universal struggle

The Revelation of John pictures the immense struggle on earth between the people of God who worship him and the people of this world who obey the forces of evil.

John envisioned what it was like to enter heaven and he describes how the Spirit took control of him, taking him into a magnificent throne room where God was surrounded by angels and people worshipping him.

Each one of the four living creatures had six wings and they were covered with eyes, inside and out. Day and night they never stopped singing:
'Holy, holy, holy, is the Lord God Almighty
    who was, who is, and who is to come.'

The four living creatures sing songs of glory and honour and thanks to the one who sits upon the throne, who lives for ever and ever. When they do so, the twenty-four elders fall down before the one who sits on the throne, and worship him who lives for ever and ever. They throw their crowns down in front of the throne and say,
'Our Lord and our God! You are worthy to receive glory, honour and power.
    For you created all things,
    and by your will they were given existence and life.6

In John's vision of heaven he saw a seven-sealed scroll, the first of a number of important symbols. Only Christ was worthy to break those seals. As each seal was broken, it revealed what was going to happen to earth. Out of the first four seals came four horsemen, one riding a white horse as a conqueror representing false peace; another, bright red, representing the wars that would occur on earth; another was a black horse representing famine;

and the fourth was a pale horse of skin and bones called death. The other three seals mention judgments that will come to the earth: of persecution, violent earthquakes and destruction, and of an awesome silence that was full of foreboding.

John then saw the people of God redeemed, with 144,000 faithful people from Israel, and behind them:

there was an enormous crowd — no one could count all the people! They were from every race, tribe, nation, and language, and they stood in front of the throne of the Lamb, dressed in white robes and holding palm branches in their hands. They called out in a loud voice: 'Salvation comes from our God, who sits on the throne, and from the Lamb!'[7]

John wrote about seven trumpets which, when blown, would reveal terrible judgments and destruction coming upon the earth. In the end, after the seventh trumpet, there would again be a cry of praise to God who was victor.

The second half of the Revelation of John tells of both the struggle on earth and of the victory that is assured through Christ. There is a tremendous spiritual battle between the forces of evil in the shape of a dragon and, in a heavenly war, the archangel Michael and his angels fight the dragon and defeat him.

Victory is already assured even though Satan is going to bring more suffering upon the people in later attacks by a terrible beast from the sea and a beast of the earth, each representing past and future empires and persecutors. Gradually the plagues and the suffering will become worse until a great battle occurs.

After seven angels bring plagues upon the earth from seven bowls, we read:

Then the spirits brought the kings together in the place that in Hebrew is called Armageddon.

Then the seventh angel poured out his bowl in the air. A loud voice came from the throne in the temple, saying, 'It is done!' There were flashes of lightning, rumblings and peals of thunder, and a terrible earthquake. There has never been such an earthquake since the creation of man; this was the worst earthquake of all! The great city was split into three parts, and the cities of all countries were destroyed . . . All the islands disappeared, all the mountains vanished. Huge hailstones, each weighing as much as fifty kilograms, fell from the sky on people, who cursed God on account of the plague of hail, because it was such a terrible plague.[8]

In John's eyes the plain of Megiddo, which had seen so many famous battles in the past, was to see the last battle of all, known as Armageddon. This would bring about the defeat of

Christ's enemies. A great victory would occur over the worst of all — Rome herself, called by her name of 'the Harlot of Babylon'. John describes it this way:

I saw another angel coming down out of heaven. He had great authority, and his splendour brightened the whole earth. He cried out with a loud voice: 'She has fallen! Great Babylon has fallen! She is now haunted by demons and unclean spirits; all kinds of filthy and hateful birds live in her. For all the nations have drunk her wine — the strong wine of her immoral lust. The kings of earth practised sexual immorality with her and the businessmen of the world grew rich from her unrestrained lust.'

. . . The kings of the earth who took part in her immorality and lust will cry and weep over the city when they see the smoke from the flames that consume her. They stand a long way off, because they are afraid of sharing in her suffering. They say, 'How terrible! How awful! This great and mighty city Babylon! In just one hour you have been punished!'

. . . Be glad, heaven, because of her destruction! Be glad, God's people and the apostles and the prophets! For God has condemned her for what she did to you![9]

So the persecutor is persecuted, and the destroyer has been utterly destroyed. The early Christians who remained faithful through the persecution saw at last the destruction of their great enemy — in a vision as yet, but soon in reality.

Each generation has seen the successors of persecuting Rome being the last enemy to be

defeated. In 1980 Francis Ford Coppola made the film *Apocalypse Now*. For him the Vietnam War was the time of the commencement of the end of the world. It wasn't. Yet anybody who reads of the present conflict through the oil-rich Middle East could see that very shortly even in our generation we could have *Apocalypse Now*.

The second coming of Jesus
The great climax is to come with the return of Jesus Christ to establish his reign and to judge the wicked. The centre of the coming of the Son of God is to be Jerusalem. John records it this way:

Then I saw heaven open, and there was a white horse. Its rider is called 'Faithful and True'. It is with justice that he judges and fights his battles. His eyes were like a flame of fire, and he wore many crowns on his head. He had a name written on him, but no-one except himself knows what it is. The robe he wore was covered with blood. His name is 'the Word of God'. The armies of heaven followed him . . . and on his thigh was written the name: 'King of kings and Lord of lords.'[10]

Just as Jesus ascended into heaven, so he will come in triumph bringing his redeemed with him who have been caught up with him in the air. Christians believe the Messiah will come victorious, when finally Satan is defeated and the world is judged.

After the return of Jesus in triumph and the establishment of his kingdom of peace and happiness, those who have

Jerusalem

opposed his word and will and who have persecuted the believers will be punished. After a final rebellious struggle, the enemies will be destroyed and Satan and his beast and false prophet will be doomed to eternal punishment. Then God will open the Book of Life and the books that record the deeds of each unrepentant sinner. Then rewards and punishments are delivered as the world is destroyed in a fiery holocaust!

Then John closes his Revelation with a great vision of the future renewal:

Then I saw a new heaven and a new earth. The first heaven and the first earth disappeared, and the sea vanished. And I saw the Holy City, the new Jerusalem, coming down out of heaven from God, prepared and ready, like a bride dressed to meet her husband. I heard a loud voice speaking from the throne: 'Now God's home is with mankind! He will live with them, and they shall be his people. God himself will be with them, and he will be their God. He will wipe away all tears from their eyes. There will be no more death, no more grief or crying or pain. The old things have disappeared.'

Then the one who sits on the throne said, 'And now I make all things new!'[11]

That is the final triumphant scene as the new Jerusalem is established with a new heaven and a new earth with the believers gathered for eternity in great joy, worshipping God and Jesus the king.

The whole book breathes a spirit of triumph and optimism as those who are being persecuted are encouraged to look to God who is still in control behind the events of the most wicked of men.

Date and time?

When is all this to happen? Every generation can see some elements of persecution and some of hope in this book for themselves, but no-one has the right to claim a timetable of their own.

The Christian has to live in obedience and expectancy for the coming of Christ. His return will be sudden, and at a point when no-one is expecting him.[12] There are some 318 allusions to the second coming of Jesus in the 260 chapters of the New Testament. Seven out of every ten chapters has some reference to the return of the Lord. He came to earth at Bethlehem in silence, submission and subjection; but the vision of his return is that he will come in power, might and glory.

So the Bible ends on a note of triumph. God's plan for humankind, expressed in creation but thwarted by man's sinfulness, was expressed through the chosen people and then through his Son, our redeemer. That same plan was told to the world by those who followed Jesus and proclaimed him as Christ. Those who have remained faithful to him will join with him when God's plan is fulfilled with a new creation of heaven and earth, the recreation of all who look for his appearing. A new people, in new bodies, in a new society, in a new universe — what a plan!

To that the Christians of the earth say: 'Amen. Even so, come, Lord Jesus.'

For personal reading

Theme: The end of time

MONDAY
The comfort of the second coming
1 Thessalonians 4:13-18

TUESDAY
The Sermon on the Mount I
Matthew 5:1-26

WEDNESDAY
The Sermon on the Mount II
Matthew 5:27-48

THURSDAY
The Sermon on the Mount III
Matthew 6:1-34 .

FRIDAY
Paul's prophecy
1 Corinthians 15:1-58

SATURDAY
The new earth
Revelation 21:1-27

SUNDAY
The truth of God's word
Revelation 22:6-21

For group study

Topic: More than conquerors

1 To what extent does the Sermon on the Mount apply to the present? To what extent does it apply to the future?

2 The Revelation of John was written in a special literary form. How is it to be interpreted?

3 What was the message of Revelation to the young church?

4 What message does the book have for us today?

5 Think back over the series and share with another person the things you have found most meaningful.

Endnotes

Chapter 1:
Peter the Disciple

1 Mark 2:14
2 Matthew 4:12-17;
   Mark 1:16-20; Mark
   2:13-17; Mark 3:20-35
3 Matthew 17:24-27;
   Mark 1:21-34; Luke
   7:1-10
4 Mark 2:1-12; John
   6:25-59
5 John 1:44; Matthew
   8:14
6 Matthew 11:20-24
7 Matthew 8:5,14-17
8 Mark 1:29
9 Matthew 17:24-27
10 Mark 1:4
11 John 1:35-42
12 Mark 1:17-18
13 Luke 5:1-10
14 Matthew 16:13-19
15 Luke 22:31-34
16 Matthew 26:69-75
17 Mark 16:7
18 1 Corinthians 15:5
19 John 21:7-19
20 Acts 1:8

Chapter 2:
Peter the Witness

1 Matthew 28:19-20
2 Deuteronomy 5:23;
   Midrash Tanchuma
   26C
3 Acts 2:1-12
4 Acts 2:14-42
5 Acts 3:6-8
6 Acts 4:13-21
7 Acts 10:12-15
8 Acts 10:22
9 Acts 11:1-18

Chapter 3:
Peter the Missionary

1 John 21:15-19
2 Acts 15:7-11; Galatians
   2:11-14
3 Galatians 1:18
4 See Galatians 2:1. It is
   not clear whether this
   was fourteen years
   after Paul's conversion
   or fourteen years after
   Paul's earlier visit.
5 Galatians 2:7,8
6 Acts 15:1
7 Acts 15:7-11
8 Acts 15:19-29
9 Acts 1:1 — 6:7
   concentrates on
   Jerusalem; Acts 6:8 —
   9:31 on Judea and
   Samaria; Acts 9:32 —
   12:24 on Antioch; Acts
   12:25 — 16:5 on
   Turkey; Acts 16:6 —
   19:20 on Europe; and
   Acts 19:21 — 28:31 on
   Rome
10 Acts 2:42; 6:7; 8:1;
   9:31; 8:14,25; 9:32-43
11 1 Peter 5:13-14; Acts
   16:6-7
12 1 Corinthians 1:12;
   Acts 18:2,12
13 Acts 2:10; Romans
   16:3-16.
14 Colossians 4:10; Acts
   15:37-39; Philemon 24;
   2 Timothy 4:11
15 Acts 12:12; Mark
   14:51,52
16 Paul Barnett, *Is the
   New Testament
   History?* Hodder and
   Stoughton, , p.84

17 Revelation 2:13; 1
   Peter 4:12 — 5:1
18 1 Peter 1:6-7; 1:11;
   2:21-23; 3:18, 4:12-15;
   2: 13-17; 4:15-17
19 1 Peter 2:20-23; 3:16;
   4:3-4
20 2 Peter 2:10-12 3:3-10;
21 This is disputed by
   some scholars who
   argue that it was the
   ending of another
   Pauline letter to
   Ephesus where he
   knew so many people
   after his three year
   ministry, rather than
   in Rome which he had
   not visited.
22 2 Timothy 4:11
23 Galatians 2:7-9; 1
   Peter 1:1

Chapter 4:
Stephen the Martyr

1 Acts 2:8-11
2 1 Corinthians 3:1-9
3 Acts 18:24-19:1
4 Abram Spiro, 'The
   Acts of the Apostles' in
   The Anchor Bible, J.
   Munk, New York,
   1967, p.284
5 F.F. Bruce in *New
   Testament History*
   warns against a too
   ready acceptance of
   Spiro's views, though
   he notes with
   appreciation 'all the
   striking affinities
   between Stephen's
   exposition and

Samaritan traditions to
which Spiro draws
attention'.
6 See *The Interpreter's
Dictionary of the
Bible*, supplementary
volume, pp.772-775
7 Acts 7:4
8 Genesis 11:32
9 Acts 7:32
10 Genesis 23:1-20; 49:31
11 Acts 7:49-50
12 Acts 7:2, 30, 35, 38,
44
13 Exodus 19 and 20;
33:11; Numbers 12:8
14 Luke 10:30-37
15 Acts 6:9-11
16 Acts 6:13,14
17 Acts 6:7
18 Acts 8:1
19 Acts 11:19,20
20 Acts 22:20
21 *Zondervan Pictorial
Encyclopaedia of the
Bible*, Vol.5, p.516
22 Galatians 1:13

Chapter 5:
James and Jude

1 Jude 1
2 Mark 6:3
3 Matthew 12:46-47;
Luke 8:19; John 2:12
4 John 7:5
5 1 Corinthians 15:7
6 Acts 12:17; 15:13;
21:18; Galatians 1:19;
Galatians 2:9,12
7 Acts 1:14
8 Matthew 13:54-57. See
also Galatians 1:29 and
1 Corinthians 9:5
9 Matthew 5:7, 34-37;
6:19; 7:16,; 20
10 James 1:4-5, 12, 13;
2:22; 4:13
11 James 1:26,27
12 James 2:14-17
13 James 2:26
14 Jude 3

Chapter 6:
Timothy and Titus

1 Galatians 2:5
2 2 Corinthians 12:18
3 2 Timothy 1:5
4 1 Timothy 3:15
5 Philippians 2:20-22
6 Romans 16:23

7 Philippians 2:19-24
8 1 Timothy 1:3-7
9 1 Timothy 4:1-2
10 1 Timothy 4:11-12
11 2 Timothy 3:16
12 1 Timothy 1:4; 4:7;
Titus 1:14
13 1 Timothy 6:5
14 2 Timothy 2:1-2
15 1 Timothy 1:11
16 2 Timothy 3:14-17
17 2 Timothy 4:8; 2
Timothy 2:5; 2
Timothy 4:6-8
18 2 Timothy 2:6; 2
Timothy 2:15-16; 23-25

Chapter 7:
The Hebrews

1 Hebrews 13:22
2 Hebrews 1:1-14; 3:1-6
3 Hebrews 3:7-4:13
4 Hebrews 4:14-5:10
5 Hebrews 7:1-10:18
6 Hebrews 10:19-25
7 Hebrews 10:19-13:17
8 Hebrews 3:6,14;
10:35,39
9 Hebrews 12:1-2
10 Hebrews 10:32-35
11 Hebrews 11:33-12:2

Chapter 8:
John

1 Mark 1:17-20
2 John 19:26
3 Matthew 27:56; Mark
15:40-41; 16:1; Luke
8:3; John 19:26
4 Acts 19:10
5 John 20:31
6 Revelation 1:9-11

Chapter 9:
The Seven Churches:
Ephesus and Smyrna

1 Revelation 1:12-18
2 1 Corinthians 15:32
3 Acts 19:8-10
4 Revelation 2:1-7
5 Revelation 2:9-10

Chapter 10:
The Seven Churches:
Pergamum and Thyatira

1 Revelation 2:12-13

2 Revelation 2:13
3 Revelation 2:14-15
4 Numbers 22-24
5 Revelation 2:16
6 Revelation 2:17
7 Revelation 2:18
8 Revelation 2:19
9 Revelation 2:20
10 Revelation 2:21
11 Revelation 2:22-23
12 Revelation 2:24-28

Chapter 11:
The Seven Churches:
Sardis, Philadelphia
Laodicea

1 Revelation 3:1
2 Matthew 23:27-28
3 Revelation 3:2-3
4 John 5:25
5 Revelation 3:3
6 Revelation 3:4-5
7 Revelation 19:14
8 Revelation 3:7-8
9 Revelation 3:9
10 Revelation 3:10-11
11 Revelation 3:12
12 Isaiah 22:22-23;
Matthew 16:19;
Matthew 28:18-20;
Hebrews 10:19-20;
Revelation 1:18
13 Colossians 4:16-17
14 Revelation 3:14
15 Revelation 3:15-16
16 Revelation 3:17
17 John 15:5
18 Revelation 3:18-19
19 Revelation 3:20-21

Chapter 12:
The Revelation
of John

1 Revelation 1:1-3
2 Revelation 1:5
3 Revelation 1:12-18;
4:6-11; 5:6-14; 19:1-7
4 Revelation 1:6-7
5 Revelation 22:18-19
6 Revelation 4:8-11
7 Revelation 7:9-10
8 Revelation 16:16-21
9 Revelation 18:1-3;
9-10; 20
10 Revelation 19:11-16
11 Revelation 21:1-5
12 Matthew 24:44;
25:1-13; Luke 21:34-36

Bibliography

Author	Title	Publisher	Date
Akurgal Ekrem	*Ancient Civilizations and Ruins of Turkey*	Kitabevi	1969
American School of Classical Studies at Athens	*The Athenian Agora*	Ekdotike Athenon	1976
Barclay William	*The Revelation of John*	St Andrews	1960
Barclay William	*The Letters of James and Peter*	St Andrews	1958
Barratt C.K. (ed.)	*The New Testament Background: Selected Documents*	SPCK	1974
Ben-Dov Meir	*In The Shadow of The Temple*	Keter	1982
Blaiklock E.M.	*The World of the New Testament*	Christian Literature Crusade	1983
Blaiklock E.M.	*The New International Dictionary of Biblical Archaeology*	Zondervan	1983
Blaiklock E.M. & Harrison R.K.	*Dictionary of Biblical Archaeology*	Zondervan	1983
Blake Everett C. & Edmonds Anna G.	*Biblical Sites in Turkey*	Redhouse	1982
Bruce F.F.	*The Book of the Acts (New International Commentary on the New Testament)*	Eerdmans	1973
Bruce F.F.	*The Epistle to the Hebrews (New International Commentary on the New Testament)*	Eerdmans	1964
Bruce F.F.	*Jesus and Christian Origins Outside the New Testament*	Hodder & Stoughton	1974
Bruce F.F.	*New Testament History*	Doubleday	1972
Bruce F.F.	*Men and Movements in the Primitive Church*	Paternoster	1979
Bruce F.F.	*The Pauline Circle*	Paternoster	1985

Author	Title	Publisher	Date
Bruce F.F.	The Spreading Flame (The Paternoster Church History) Vol.1	Paternoster	1958
Cornfield Gaalyah	Archaeology of the Bible	Harper & Row	1976
Dehan Emmanuel	Megiddo: Armageddon	Dehan	1980
Douglas J.D. et. al. (eds)	The Illustrated Bible Dictionary	IVP	1980
Douglas J.D.	New Testament History	IVP	1972
Drane John	The Life of the Early Church	Lion	1982
Eliades G.S.	The House of Dionysus	Hannibal	
Gaebelein Frank E. (ed.)	The Expositers Bible Commentary (Vol.2)	Eerdmans	1978
Goldsworthy Graeme	The Gospel in Revelation	Paternoster	1984
Green Michael	Evangelism in the Early Church	Eerdmans	1980
Green Michael	The Second Epistle of Peter and the Epistle of Jude	Eerdmans	1973
Guidebook	The Catacombs of Rome and the Origins of Christianity		
Gundry Robert H.	A Survey of the New Testament	Zondervan	1970
Guthrie Donald	New Testament Introduction	IVP	1970
Hendriksen W.	More than Conquerors	IVP	1962
Josephus	Antiquities of the Jews and Jewish Wars	Pickering and Inglis	1963
Loffreda Stanislao	A Visit to Capernaum	Franciscan Press	1983
Martin Hugh	Simon Peter	Banner of Truth	1967
Meinardus Otto	St John of Patmos and the Seven Churches of the Apocalypse	Lycabettus	1974
Meinardus Otto	St Paul in Ephesus and the Cities of Galatia & Cyprus	Lycabettus	1973
Morris Leon	The Gospel according to John (New International Commentary on the New Testament)	Eerdmans	1971
Munch Johannes	The Acts of The Apostles (The Anchor Bible)	Doubleday	1967
Onen Dr U.	Ephesus, Ruins & Museum	Akodemia	1983
Packer, Tenney and White (eds.)	The World of the New Testament	Nelson	1982
Packer, Tenney and White (eds.)	The Bible Almanac	Nelson	1980
Papathanassopoulos G.	The Acropolis	Krene	1977
Phillips J.B.	Letters to the Young Churches	Geoffrey Bles	1947
Ramsay William M.	The Letters to the Seven Churches	Hodder & Stoughton	1904
Rogerson John	The New Atlas of The Bible	Macdonald	1985
Stedman Ray	Acts 1-12: Birth of the Body	Vision	1974
Stibbs A.M.	Peter: A Commentary	Tyndale	1966

Author	Title	Publisher	Place	Date
Stevenson J. (ed.)	*A New Eusebius*	SPCK		1968
Stott John R.W.	*Epistles of John (Tyndale New Testament Commentaries)*	Tyndale		1964
Tasker R.V.G.	*James*	Tyndale		1957
Tenney Merrill C.	*New Testament Times*	Nelson		1965
Tenney Merrill C. (ed.)	*Pictorial Encyclopaedia of The Bible*	Zondervan		1976
Themelis Petros G.	*Ancient Corinth*	Hannibal		
Thompson J.A.	*Handbook of Life in Bible Times*	Intervarsity Press		1986
Unger Merrill F.	*Archaeology and the New Testament*	Eerdmans		1962
Yadin Yigael	*The Temple Scroll*	Weidenfeld & Nicholson		1985
Yamauchi E.	*The World of the First Christians*	Lion		1981
Yamauchi E.	*The Interpreter's Dictionary of the Bible (5 Vols)*	Abingdon		1976

Video cassettes

This book is based on the film series, originally screened on major television networks in Australia and available on video. For further details of the video series, please write to:

TRA Productions
Wesley Central Mission
210 Pitt Street
Sydney, NSW 2000
Australia

Phone (02) 267 8741

All Bible passages are from the *Good News Bible* (American Bible Society edition).